FIGHT FOR YOUR
Fairytale

A Guided Quest to Total Transformation

COLLEEN H. OCHAB

For more information, email connect@colleenochab.com.

ISBN: 979-8-89694-842-1 - Hardcover

ISBN: 979-8-89694-733-2 - eBook

ISBN: 979-8-89694-734-9 - Paperback

A Token To Aid You On Your Adventure!

Welcome, traveler! To say thank you for purchasing my book, I would like to offer you a special token to aid you on your adventure. To get the best experience with this book, I've found readers who download and use my *Fight For Your Fairytale Companion Guide* are able to implement the tactics faster to set their new adventure into motion in their real lives.

You can get your printable PDF copy by visiting:
colleenochab.com/fairytalecompanionguide

To my Game Master, Elizabeth,
thank you for introducing me to a game that
changed, and probably saved, my life.
Every session is a blessing.

Table of Contents

Level Zero - The Backstory

Lost: No Map & No Idea Where to Go Next 7

Part 1: The Internal Journey

Level One - Inspiration Hits

Commitment to Exploration 27

Level Two - Your Current Inventory

What Holds Us Back & Propels Us Forward 41

Level Three - Deficiencies

Grow or Discard What's Complicated...............................57

Level Four - Proficiencies

Lean Into What Comes Naturally 69

Level Five - The Shopkeep

The Shiny & The Useful..79

Level Six - Health Potions

Stocking Up For When You Need It Most........................91

Level Seven - The Tavern

Q&A = Quests & Advice...103

Level Eight - NPCs

The Power of Weak Ties...111

Level Nine - Mentor

A Guide Beyond Measure 121

Level Ten - Align

Mindset: Your Closest Friend or Greatest Foe...................131

Part 2: The Pursuit of Adventure

Level Eleven - Beginning the Adventure
A Purpose in Mind & Moving Forward 145

Level Twelve - Building Your Party
Finding Your People 153

Level Thirteen - Experience Points
Craft Your Tracking System 163

Level Fourteen - Collecting Your Bounties
The Reward of Success, Even a Small One................................173

Level Fifteen - Staking Your Vampires
Sometimes the Suckers Need to Get Dealt With 181

Level Sixteen - Surprise, You Died
Death: Life's Greatest Teacher 191

Level Seventeen - Realign
Priorities Change, Time to Readjust............................201

Level Eighteen - Respawn
A New Lease on Life 209

Level Nineteen - Conquering Your BBEG
Meeting Your Big (Brillant) (Expanding) (Goal) 217

Level Twenty - On To Your Next Horizon
What's Your Next Fairytale? 227

The Adventure Recap
Resources & Acknowledgements 233

A Note from the Author:

Fight for your fairytale; it does exist.

If you pull one thing away from the reading of this book, I hope it is this.

This book is designed to help open your eyes to areas of personal growth through the spyglass of role-playing games, video games, fiction books, and fantasy movies. In particular, I often speak through the lens of role-playing games, from here on often noted as RPG, because it is what instigated my personal journey of self-discovery and the writing of this book.

If you are not yet a fan of RPGs, perhaps this will tip the scales and encourage you to take the leap into your first adventure, but that is not at all the point of this book. Whether or not role-playing games are inside your regular repertoire on game night, I think you will find the storytelling nature of this book as a refreshing twist on your usual self-growth book. I hope the parallels and examples included from other video games, fiction books, TV shows, and fantasy movies will satisfy those who have not yet endeavored in the realm of role-playing games.

Beginning to play my first RPG campaign and diving headlong into listening to the *Critical Role* podcast started a trajectory of change in my life that I never expected. I hope it can for you as well.

Many RPGs offer a supplementary "game master's guide" to help you understand the rules of the game and move forward with satisfaction. May this book serve as a "game master's guide" for building your real-life fairytale. May it open your eyes to new ideas and give you a small handbook to begin to make the changes you are yearning for in life.

You deserve to have *your* fairytale exist.

At the same time, this book is not a magic potion. You cannot drop some gold in an oddities shop for it and suddenly dissolve all your problems. Our problems cannot be solved magically. In real life, we don't always have all the agency and control, but perhaps the stories contained within can be a salve to restore some health points and give you the courage to start taking some pointed action. That's the "fight" portion of the title.

No fight is easy. Not all fights have a satisfactory ending, but we are warriors, and we will choose to fight nonetheless. Why? Because we owe it to ourselves to try.

To do so, I encourage you to become the game master. What does this mean? It is the role of the game masters to create a unique world for the player characters to live in inside an RPG campaign. So, too, is it our responsibility to build the world around us.

Claiming the role of game master, we acknowledge the personal responsibility we need to take to cause change in our own lives. There is no one else to swoop in and do that for us—even if we would like that! Guilty romance book lover here. I hear you!

In these pages, we recognize it is our responsibility to discover our faults and biases, as well as work to better ourselves. And I cannot stress this enough: ourselves only.

We cannot seek to change others. As a new game master and even new player quickly learns, the reality is we cannot control the other player characters or even the non-player characters in our stories—which can make for some pleasant, and some unpleasant, surprises. This release of control can be difficult. So it is important to remember, everyone grows up differently: physically where we live; the situations we experienced as children and adults; the education we received, or did not; the amount of money we have; and the roles we have chosen or been forced to play. So, seek to give others grace and give yourself even more. You are a growing and constantly learning human being. I am a big believer that sometimes we need to have a space to fail. It is through failure that we can learn and grow. This is your space to make some of those positive failures.

My hope is that you can take this book to heart and allow it to help you transform the way you face off with the challenges of life. I hope at the end of this book your journey has taken you somewhere new and exciting, with a fresh optimistic mindset to go alongside it.

That being said, while I hope transformation is here between these pages for you, please take care of yourself first.

We often use role-playing games, video games, TV shows, books, and movies to escape our realities for a moment. As a writer and screenwriter, I thank you for enjoying and supporting the work my fellow artists and I create. However, while these pieces of art are fun and ultimately beneficial, I will also be encouraging you to use these "stories" and "games" as tools to explore your real-life struggles and even minor (or major) traumas. It depends what you are up for!

Some things in this book may bring up tough feelings. I encourage you to seek to understand these "negatives" as a chance to build more positives. Nevertheless, if you are feeling intensely discouraged or down or depressed, please turn to trusted party members, family, friends, or a therapist to assist you.

You are not alone.

Most of this book is my opinion—a series of actions, reflections, and mindsets I have developed and cultivated for myself to look at the struggles of life in a new way—and that I am choosing to share with you in case it might be a benefit. I'm a fairly positive and optimistic person, but I've been in the dark, too. There were days I barely wanted to get out of bed. As I said prior, YOU are the game master of your own life. In the end, it is not MY OPINION but YOURS that matters. You get the final call. Take what assists you. Leave what doesn't. This is about your journey.

As a warning to all my readers, this book contains real-life stories of trauma as well as fictional ones. In particular, my own stories of hardship, including a personal fight with breast cancer in my twenties, mirrored in my character's bouts with death, loss, anger, and violence. Please prepare yourself if these topics can be triggering for you. If you find it to be too much, please part with this book in peace knowing that I send you away with love, my complete respect, and my endless desire that you will be able to handle the challenges in your own life and learn to thrive beyond them. YOU deserve your fairytale.

I am looking forward to walking on this journey with you. I hope I can become one of your trusted party members, or at least a memorable NPC (non-player character) who helped and guided you on your quest through life. I look forward to hearing what you discover, for even I am giving in to the reality of being the game master, the creator of this book. You, my player, are going to discover, create, and surprise me more than I realize yet. I look forward to every moment.

Now let's begin.

Lost: No Map & No Idea Where to Go Next

> *"The dark night of the soul comes*
> *just before revelation.*
> *When everything is lost, and all seems darkness,*
> *then comes the new life and all that is needed."*

FROM JOSEPH CAMPBELL'S REFLECTIONS
ON THE ART OF LIVING

You walk deep inside the heart of a forest. All around the trees are dense, rough, and textured closeup, but fade away quickly to indistinct blues, purples, and eventually blacks the farther you look on into the tree line. You cannot make out anything in the hanging boughs above, let alone the open sky, which you haven't seen in days. Oh, how you are craving to see the sun!

There is a creeping, chilled fog lingering low to the ground, which is making your clothes feel damp. Perhaps you are more than a little ill-prepared. You should have brought a thicker cloak for a modicum of comfort, but your pack is heavy enough as it is.

All around the forest is quiet besides the snap of your steps on the ground below and the gentle puff of your breath from your lungs. Far away, you can hear the eerie caw of a raven, or maybe two.

The path is difficult to follow; if there is even a path at all. It is steep and angled in places, traversing the pass of a mountain, covered in overgrown roots and sticks. There are clumps of slick moss and thickets of weeds. You find your worn leather boots slipping on the uneven footing, or even getting caught up in the underbrush, which makes your heart race with the thought of sliding off an unseen cliff somewhere just beyond your course.

You had thought, leaving the organized road behind, that this part of your adventure was something you were more than prepared for. You have many skills that you were told would prepare you for the journey ahead. But never did you think, with such a focused future, that you could get lost—let alone *be lost*.

Now you find yourself losing motivation and drive. None of this is like you thought it would be. Why hadn't your teachers given you a map? Or warned you of the swampy ground you passed a day before? Or the traveling pack of wolves you hid from in the trees overnight and then scuffed your knee falling back to the ground the next morning?

You are physically tired. Your muscles are aching, and your brain is yearning for a place to rest securely. Your sense of purpose has fallen away. All through your head run thoughts you cannot control. What was all the hard work for if you were just going to flounder and maybe die here in the woods? Where are all your so-called friends now that you are facing one of the biggest challenges of your life? Were you even meant to adventure like this at all?

In the fierceness of the terrain, the terror of unforeseen dangers, and the loneliness of the road, all remembrance of your dreams and goals have faded away like the sun setting beyond the mountains somewhere you cannot see.

Another night is upon you, and you are feeling quite hopeless.

What are you going to do now?

Funny how that scene is probably so relatable to a moment in your life, right? Maybe a moment you experienced in the past. Or hopefully, one you are experiencing right now. I say hopefully, yes. Because if you are in the thick of that fog, I've found you at the perfect time.

A time when you are ready to take action, because there is no turning back now. A time when you are ready to step beyond your previous boundaries because you realize they are limiting your ability to dream. A time when you are ready to be open to new things for the sheer sake of taking a glorious chance. A time when you are ready to set down the baggage you may have been clinging to for years because you realize, without it, you might be able to fly.

It's okay if this time is also one of fear. What if you aren't ready? What if you don't know how to proceed? What if something is preventing you from moving forward? Just like your character moves through the forest wondering if they are ill-equipped because they forgot a thicker cloak, what if you are ill-equipped to handle what comes next? These are all valid questions, but as I said before, you are in the thick of the woods, so let's explore a way through rather than stand still, paralyzed with the "what ifs." Take my hand. Breathe. I'm here to walk alongside you.

I can almost guarantee that at some point in your life, and likely more than once, whether you are in your teens, twenties, forties, or seventies, you have felt lost. You have felt stuck in some daunting situation. You have felt you were not moving in the direction you were destined to go, but your compass was broken. I know that was me less than a year before pulling the proverbial trigger and deciding to write this book.

It doesn't matter that you live a normal life and in fact aren't a medieval fantasy adventurer. You have a fog-filled, densely-forested mountain pass in your life. Just think of the explosion of unknowns in 2020 as an example. I could list a hundred mountains I climbed in the years following the onset of the pandemic: the loss of a job I loved, the isolation from loved ones, the fear of war and violence, and the unknown of drastic inflation, just to name a few. It was surreal. It was like staring at a crossroads trying to make a choice with no knowledge of where that choice would lead.

Feeling lost is one of the worst feelings in the world. Sadly, it is also one of the most common. What walks hand in hand with feeling lost? Perhaps depression, anxiety, isolation, fear, hopelessness, and negativity walk beside you—a cold, foreboding presence that steals away your dreams, hopes, and desires for the future. A vampire that drains you and leaves you empty with no goal to move forward to and no desire to find one.

You have lost your fairytale in the middle of the woods. You are starting to believe it does not exist, or even worse, that you don't deserve to find it.

We have all experienced a moment in life when we are lost and are not sure how to move ahead. It is our personal "la noche oscura del alma" or "dark night of the soul" where we are starting to give up hope and are losing our belief in the fairytale. We feel abandoned by the world, by society, and maybe even by friends and family as we travel in isolation.

Maybe we feel abandoned by ourselves.

So as you move forward, let this idea comfort you. There are adventurers all over the world who are in the same position as you—in a different location, a different timezone, and a different life situation—but those distant adventurers are all fighting for the same thing. We are a community of people who are fighting for the fairytale in our own personal lives just like the epic heroes in our favorite books and movies.

That is exactly what I intend to teach you. Through stories, my musings, and our adventuring together, I hope to equip you with the tools to reconcile with the past, claim a new present, and just in case this moment happens again in your future—which it will, because that's just the way life goes—lay the foundation to escaping your next dark forest faster and easier than ever before. You will discover (or rediscover) your personal fairytale. You will begin to take action toward achieving it.

This may sound like a big vow to deliver, but I can only say it's true because I have done it. I've been through the darkest of the dark of my life thus far, and I have chosen to put it behind me. No one can be positive twenty-four hours a day, seven days a week; however, we can recognize when the shadows are creeping in, acknowledge them, and use tactics we've developed to fight them away. I myself have used my RPG character, as well as my favorite novels and movies, as a magnifying glass for self-introspection in interludes to my bouts of escapism. It has changed my life. Not only that, but I have seen it change and improve the lives of those close to me.

In this book, step-by-step, we will explore what it means to be the game master of your real life. At first, it is a bit like a crutch to help you move forward. We lean heavily on our favorite characters, whether from our personal RPG campaigns, fiction books, or fantasy movies, to teach us and inspire us. You will come to acknowledge what you have learned from them that you may be ignoring, including the tools and strategies to pull yourself out of any despondence, downheartedness, or distress in your life. As the inspiration and motivation grows, you will embody the epic hero, even in the dullest moments of life. Even in the toughest moments of life. You will be empowered to grow further and deeper. You will embrace and fight for your fairytale, and suddenly even a tough life won't seem so dark. Then, when you are on your own two feet again, those characters who are close to your heart will become the friends who travel alongside you, forever entertaining you and filling you with joy. They walk beside you because warriors walk together.

So, who even is this game master creating the adventure before you right now? While most of the time the player characters (aka the people who live in the game master's world) learn very little about the omniscient voice that pulls the strings, I think it is important for you to know a bit more about me.

My name is Colleen. At the time of writing this book, I am in my late twenties counting the days instead of the years to my thirties. I am transitioning from living with a handful of roommates to finding that first apartment with my partner to beginning to house hunt. What a crazy time in one's life, no? Your roots, once wide, now slowly growing deep. I am a college graduate with a bachelor's degree under my belt, am currently attending an MFA program in screenwriting, and have been working for over ten years in corporate businesses both big and small. Some epic adventurer, huh? Hi, call me 'cubicle junkie'!

My discovery of "fighting for the fairytale" began in my own dark night of the soul. Despite a great many things being wonderful in my life (a privilege some are not so lucky to have), it felt like my compass was broken. I was feeling lost. I did not have direction on where I was going next. I was walking blindly down a path toward an unknown destination. I was disconnected from my passions. My goals were superficial and short-sighted. Yep, I was feeling near despondent, totally downhearted, and filled with a distress I just couldn't identify. I couldn't put a name on what this fog was. I was so deep, I couldn't separate the forest from the trees.

The pandemic of 2020 thrust me, like so many, out of the comfort zone of a workplace I had been at for five years. I was unemployed for six months, at first because I thought the pandemic would end and I would get called back to work in a few short weeks, but then later because jobs in my industry were hard to come by. Entertainment was not exactly happening amid the shutdown. I ended up in a job I enjoyed (and was good at), thankfully. However, stepping outside of entertainment, I was no longer living quite as purposefully toward my original "goals" as I felt I had been before. I had deviated from where I thought I was going and frankly did not have a new goal of where I even wanted to end up. The fairytale was becoming muddled.

The following year or two were full of "being busy" and wore down my resilience and positivity. To be honest, I did not have the mental strength to manage the onslaught of negative emotions. On the outside, I pretended. But inside, I was floundering. I grew irritable and prone to outbursts of anger or tears. I had a strong feeling that I was not WHO I was supposed to be, WHERE I was supposed to be, or DOING what I was supposed to be doing. I was at a major crossroads of my life feeling MAJORLY lost. And yes, you guessed it, no roadmap in sight. As a person who loves directions, rules, and a checklist, this feeling that there was no guide and no map was utterly devastating to me. I couldn't grasp the purpose of my life, making me feel useless, and the vibrant colors were fading.

Where I was may be relatable to your situation. Just a breathing person, following the motions of a life, trying to do adult things like work and pay the bills, yet somehow feeling out of place. My love of self-growth books was doing me a whole lot of good—filling the pages of notebooks with quotes I would never re-read! I could not crack down on any habit I wanted to implement, frequently finding myself back at square one. I had an all-or-nothing mentality that gave in to nothing an awful lot. I remember the voice in my head calling myself lazy, unmotivated, or lacking resolve. I see now, looking back, that was probably the voice of a society I was so keen to "please" at the time, drowning out my true voice inside.

I was looking for something to click and nothing did.

At a time when nothing was going right in my story, I did anything I could to escape into the stories of others. I am so lucky that other people's stories were there for me when I was in the darkest part of my forest. Those stories caught me and held me up, like a life vest in the middle of the ocean. I deep-dived into fantasy novels—rediscovering my love of reading (thank you, Bookstagram), rewatched my favorite epic movies (hello, *Lord of the Rings* and *Pirates of the Caribbean*), explored new Korean dramas and animes, and of course, began my glorious ascent into the world of role-playing games.

I will admit I am a fairly new fan of RPGs. I started listening to *Critical Role* at the behest of my best friends only in 2020 shortly before we tried our first one-shot game. I fell hard and fell fast. I ended up listening to over 20,000 minutes that year, a trend that continued on into 2021 and beyond, if that helps give you a good picture. So began my transformation at the hands of fantasy.

I repeat it again. I am so lucky that I was introduced to RPGs at that moment of my life. Struggling mentally with just about everything, the glory of game night suddenly became THE THING that kept me going. Every week, my three college roommates joined me for several hours in a campaign via Discord. At one point, we were located in three different time zones! I loved our games and the time we spent together.

It was not just escapism; it was a *necessity*.

I was picking up on something I hadn't felt in a long time: creativity and inspiration.

Playing weekly games with my best friends and crafting my character awoke a fire in me that had long gone dark and cold. I realized my character was intelligent, creative, and complicated— just like me. Yet, she was everything I also wanted to become—bold, passionate, and strong. I decided I wanted to become more like her. In doing so, many of the tactics, strategies, actions, and reflections of this book were born.

Despite reading dozens of self-growth books, it took embodying my RPG character, Mereoleona (Leona) Valerien, the high elf druid bounty hunter, to actually put the tactics from the self-growth books into habits in my real life. Letting Leona be the voice in my head rather than society, she pointed out how happy reading made me feel. This reinvigorated my childhood passion for fantasy books and forced me to commit to actually sitting down to write my own—surprise, surprise, it's her story. Knowing she trains every day with her sword and magic, Leona motivated me to get back in the gym, reminding me that I had the skill and determination to be a fighter, too. I hit my 100 lbs bench goal that year. She told me persistently that it was my responsibility to find, rekindle, and pursue my own dreams. Even though she was going to walk beside me, she couldn't choose the path. I had to. That was the first time I wrote down: "Fight for the Fairytale; it does exist."

A long, long time ago, I wanted to become a storyteller and a filmmaker. I started writing my passion series in the third grade and dreamed of one day seeing it play on the silver screen. Yet, I put that on the back burner year after year. I always treated it more like a hobby, even when my English teacher in my freshman year of high school said, "You're writing a novel? I want to read it." During my undergrad, I skirted around the dream, too, by pursuing a double major in Communications and Digital Media and Theatre Production. Despite snagging good roles as a Marketing Specialist after graduation, the positions in my job search started to drift to cinematographer, editor, and producer. Yet again, I scolded myself for being foolish and hastily would close the internet browser window.

I don't know why it took eighteen years for me to realize that I should just pursue being the writer my third grade childhood self wanted to become. I guess it always seemed like a pipe-dream rather than a career—hanging out in the periphery. I lied to myself that it was logic, that I could not make writing my income or my life's work (even though other people had). Unsurprisingly, Leona too had the bad habit of doing what she thought society expected of her, rather than following her heart.

It took being diagnosed with breast cancer at the age of twenty-six for the switch to flip for both of us.

The dreaded call—you have cancer. It was one of the shortest calls ever. I remember the doctor even using the formal name, malignant carcinoma, instead of just telling me outright. I was at work and literally had to Google search to confirm. I broke down in a mess of tears, and my coworkers found out even before my mom, my partner, or my best friends, but don't worry, Leona learned first, standing beside me through every moment. This time though, I feared not even Leona could pull me out of the darkness I saw looming on the horizon.

Suddenly my life was a mess of appointments, trying to figure out the what, when, and how of treatment. Cancer put my life on total pause when I was in the driver seat with Leona shotgun begging and yearning to move forward.

The reason people hate cancer is because, like a rogue in the night, it appears to steal time, not only the time it takes to undergo treatment, but the risk of it taking a lifetime in a matter of months or years. However, cancer also *gave* me time. While it was an experience I wish upon no one, cancer shut everything else down so I had "quiet" to discover where I wanted to go next when I had been too "busy" to even previously consider. A blessing in disguise.

Not only that, but I already had Leona at my back. I was attuned to listening to her advice. When I was waging war in my brain, she held my head in her lap while I cried, kept me positive, and helped me to see that this horrible fight was going to transform me beyond anything I ever imagined. She lifted my head above the surface of the water when the negative questions started to spiral into a drowning storm.

If Leona could move forward after her family life was destroyed by vampires and make her way in the world, why could I not defeat cancer and move on to a better life? A life I truly wanted? I fought hard to stay positive when I wanted to throw in the towel and be pissed. It was such a hard struggle, several years of fighting, but I found myself again, and I unearthed a me that had long been buried through sheer persistence and will. I found my true heart—the heart of a writer—one who's going to show up every day never knowing if readers are even going to get their hands on her book, and in the end, not really caring. Writing filled me with joy and passion, and that was all that mattered.

With a sudden awareness of my own mortality, I realized life was too short, and my passion for writing was too big. I owed it to myself and the world to see my stories come to life on the page and the screen. In the form of a heartbreaking, ugly-crying, quarter-life cancer crisis, I decided to fully dedicate myself to writing my books and applied to graduate school for screenwriting even in the midst of the fog of chemotherapy. At the time, it was physically the hardest thing to do. But with Leona's strength by my side, I knew the next fall I would be beyond cancer, and I would want to take action and move forward. Today, I am so glad I fought in that difficult moment.

And so, I had a sudden new fairytale to fight for. It was scarier than any leap I had ever attempted before, because for the first time I was taking a risk that was so close to my heart. I truly realized that I had stepped so far away from being the storyteller in my own life, and here I was taking the pen back in my hand.

I am no expert at this, nor a famous author, yet, but I am someone who is genuinely walking the hard road, fighting to make my fairytale a reality. I see my character, Leona, as this extension of myself, but a version of me far more powerful and more capable of handling what is going on in my life. Just like me, she is fraught with faults. Real. I am living more like her, learning from her. I hope through this book to show you how to do the same—with your own heart characters, your own journey, and your own fairytale.

You might be coming to this book because you are an avid fan of RPGs and saw that dragon on the cover—self-proclaimed, loud-and-proud, fantasy nerd!

Maybe you have never read a self-growth book in your life. I hope my storytelling style and the fairytale, RPG, book, and movie analogies will pique your interest and help you stick around. I promise it will be worth it when you see your life begin to change in ways you never imagined.

If you do not know much about RPGs, but have a mild interest from things you have heard from friends or on the internet, and you are in search of a self-growth book that speaks to you in a different way, well, welcome traveler.

Or maybe you are somewhere in between. No matter where you are, I have a feeling this book can speak to you. Not only speak to you, but change you.

I have a feeling I know what you are thinking. How do I combine self-improvement and getting healthier in mind and body with being nerdy? The two really don't align in today's society, especially in American culture. The media portrays fit people as athletes who are definitely not the nerdy type. And don't get me started on the amount of chubby, out-of-touch nerds they put in TV shows and movies. But stereotypes don't define us, right?

I like to use myself as an example. I love everything nerdy, but you can also find me in the gym. Does anyone feel like a tough workout and heading home to make a meal out of one of our favorite fantasy novels? I'm your gal. To touch a very niche audience here: you can bet Nesta from *A Court of Silver Flames* by Sarah J. Maas helps me get through every single stair climber workout! If Nesta can climb 10,000 rough-hewn stairs to prove to herself she's a strong, capable woman who can achieve whatever she sets her determination toward, I can handle a few hundred stairs on a machine in an air-conditioned gym. But I digress.

I have found nerdy people to be some of the most "in touch with reality" people I have ever met, despite their minds being lost in the clouds of their current favorite fantasy series. Nerds often have extreme self-awareness. Awareness of the world. Awareness of people. I think that can exacerbate anxiety and depression when the world doesn't match what we hope it will be.

But you know what? We nerdy types are also very willing to explore therapy. We seek to improve ourselves, even if it's challenging sometimes. I guess that is one of the reasons you have your hands, or ears, on this book.

So has fantasy changed your life yet?

If you are three hundred sessions deep in an RPG campaign, I am assuming the answer is yes, in that you have dedicated a lot of your precious personal time to it, but I don't think it has shown you everything it can yet.

I invite you to explore further in this book. Here we venture to explore RPGs, video games, books, and movies on a deeper level. We will explore everything the characters within have to teach us. We will acknowledge our strengths and our weaknesses. And, most importantly, we will learn what it means to play the game master in our real lives. We are going to discover and build a fairytale that is unique to us.

You will come to acknowledge what else you have learned from fiction that you may have been ignoring, including the tools and strategies to pull you out of any funk in your life, no matter how serious or silly, and empower you to grow further, even when the going is tough.

Personal growth is challenging. It requires us to look at ourselves on a deeper level and face the demons that we normally like to hide from everyone, including ourselves. It takes acknowledging our weaknesses, but it also will highlight our strengths.

So, what has happened since I started embracing fantasy as a motivator and a guide in my real life? It took so much fighting, day in and day out, to get here. Over time, all that hard work and dedication started to pay off.

First of all, I committed to writing this book. I said fiercely, my fairytale includes becoming a published author, and I made it happen. My coach will tell you that I set some hard deadlines for myself. Some that I hit and some that I missed, and missed by a LONG SHOT! However, the pride that this story is out in the world is beyond anything I ever hoped. The community growing around it is an even more unexpected and welcome surprise.

While writing this book, I found my loving partner. Someone who committed to me fully from the earliest moments, even when I was diagnosed with breast cancer before we even celebrated our one year anniversary. He could have packed his bags in a moment, but instead, he hunkered down for the fight right alongside me. Like Leona, finding the right person meant I didn't have to be the powerful one all the time. There was someone else in my world willing to take a watch and take out a few bad guys. Not everyone is going to meet that person in life, and knowing that reminds me to be grateful this element of life is a part of my story.

In October of 2023, my partner proposed. With his support as well as the support of my larger party—my parents, my best friends, and our two beautiful (yet complicated) rescue dogs—I fought beyond cancer and entered into this new era of self. I am grateful every day to have the privilege to know them. They were by my side through my dark night of the soul, my cancer journey, and beyond. I am excited to share the next life experiences that come with them—hopefully many more happy ones than difficult or tragic.

I now can call myself 100% cancer-free! I have completed six rounds of numbing chemotherapy, a painful double mastectomy, the daily discomfort of radiation, and reconstruction surgery, which was surprisingly easy after everything else. While we continue to monitor, I am excited to be back to an active life not dictated by the fatigue-inducing cycles of chemo. My progress back to the gym is slow, but day by day, my body is growing stronger, and Leona encourages me to show up even on days I have to crawl rather than run. We modify and adjust to my new body, but at least lifting is back in my life.

As I said before, in the midst of the dark night of my treatment, I applied to graduate school and even had the epiphany that I wanted to become a full-time author and screenwriter—changing my major completely in the middle of the application process! I am working toward my MFA in Screenwriting at DePaul University while writing these pages and should be a proud graduate by the time it is in your hands. School keeps me very busy alongside my full-time job and my continued habit of writing every day. Jokingly in my social media videos, when I teach about what I am learning, I say, "I'm going to grad school so you don't have to." But to be honest, I love to learn and

I have always wanted a master's degree. My professors and cohort are some of my greatest cheerleaders. So if you want to go to school and have the means to do so, you absolutely should take the leap. Every moment is a dream for me. Perhaps that is a fairytale for you as well.

Thanks to writing and storytelling, my life is filled with infinitely more happiness! My nine-to-five job is even more pleasurable knowing I also have an outlet to my creativity and my lifelong dreams in the five-to-nine portions before and after the work day. If you enjoy the storytelling aspects of this book, I hope you will look out for my medieval fantasy fiction novels. Leona, whom you already met, and Lake, my shapeshifting protagonist of my third grade passion series, are waiting to meet you. Bug me to write faster!

Who knows what else has happened by the time you have this book in your hands! Fingers crossed the adventure continues in an epic way!

I have yet to see where my journey will take me in the end, but the concepts within this book continuously stay a part of my daily life. I try to implement and practice them on my quest to better myself and make my fairytale a reality. I've worked so hard to get here, and as things start to fall into place, I know there will be more mountains ahead. Yet, I know I am better equipped to traverse them. Understand—these concepts I will present to you can be found in many other places—other self-help books, motivational speeches, and grit paragon success stories, but it took seeing them through the light of my RPG character to actually root itself deeply. I hope the same can be true for you.

If you embark on the journey of this book, letting yourself dive in and truly trust the process, I vow that you will feel a sense of empowerment, clarity, and hope that perhaps you have never experienced before. All your favorite fantasies—whether books or games or movies—will be more than just an escape, but an inspiration. Perhaps, over time, while taking to heart the core tenets of this book, you will not call them an escape at all, but a pleasure.

This is no time to wait. You are already in the thick of the forest. Sunset has come and gone, and now the night is growing. Shadows are everywhere.

Yes, though there is no map, no mentor, nor party members by your side, you continue and press on into the night, gritting your teeth when the hoot of an owl spooks you from overhead.

Despite being lost, you refuse to turn back. In the journey ahead, you will step into your power and begin to fight for the fairytale. And not just any fairytale, but *yours*.

PART ONE

The Internal Journey

Commitment to Exploration

*"For my part I know nothing with any certainty,
but the sight of the stars
makes me want to dream."*

FROM VINCENT VAN GOGH

Sunset has come and gone. You only know this because the woods have grown intensely dark again. Instead of eerily cast shadows, there is darkness everywhere. You keep your eyes down, watching your feet to avoid branches and other things that might make you take a tumble. You can only see that much, only a little bit. It's a wonder you can see at all, but it's probably because you haven't lit a fire in days. Your eyes have adjusted to the perpetual lack of light.

If you let your mind wander, you see figures and silhouettes out of your peripheral vision. You know it has to be your mind playing tricks on you, but fears that once seemed childish now feel oppressive and immediate. Demons and monsters lurk, not from under your bed, but setting traps, lying in wait for you just beyond your limited vision.

You feel your heart begin to race.

Your thoughts quicken to make pace.

Yes, you were a fool. You should have stayed home. It would have been safer than this perpetual sense of anxiety. It would have been better to ignore the dreams. It would have been easier to just chug along like everyone else.

But there was nothing for you back there either.

That was why you headed out in the first place.

You stew. Ugh, it's like having two tiny people on your shoulders, constantly arguing. In the end, neither of them is solving your problem. You're still lost.

Another hoot of an owl stirs you from your internal dialogue. Your head whips to the beady golden eyes that flash in the darkness. Your stomach is in your throat, but the feathered animal just hoots again and sails off farther into the trees.

Okay, okay, enough. It's time to settle down somewhere for the night.

Out of the corner of your eye, you catch another flash of light. It could just be your brain imagining things, but you swear the trees look different over there, off your course. Somehow the silhouettes of the trees look like they're glowing.

Would it hurt to go look? You are so lost, you have nothing to lose.

Stepping carefully from the game trail you are following, you walk toward the glowing. It is not much, but the trees are indeed lit differently here than the rest of the forest.

Climbing through bracken, you are met with some large boulders, stacked one over the other. They block your path like a wall, and the trees have grown over them, but the glowing persists. Yes, some light is definitely there.

Carefully you shimmy up the first boulder, clutching to vines and roots. You find some more handholds and a few indents to place your feet. You pull yourself up.

You push through the tree branches. A few scratch your face, but the rest you are able to push away. The light is growing, and suddenly, climbing up the face of another steep rock, your head pops out of the tree line.

The heavy boughs that have loomed overhead for days disappear.

Your eyes are so poorly adjusted to any form of light that you blink heavily. It makes your eyes water. Above you is the jet-black night.

This rocky little hill above the trees gives you a glimpse for miles of the forest surrounding you. Though the tops of the trees are as black as the night above, the scene is breathtaking.

Millions of stars sparkle down on you. The stars seem to wink and shimmer. A million tiny fairies, dancing far away in the sky. You have seen stars before, but never this way. Never before have you been so high up, so close to the sky. Never before were you surrounded by such emptiness. No city lamps or fires for miles and miles.

Perhaps this is what it was all for. Days of hiking in overgrown forest, the sunlight barely leaking through the trees. All the nights where the shadows grew thick. All so your eyes could adjust. All so you could prepare to experience this sudden sense of wonder. All so you could have gratitude for the light.

You set down your pack and settle down on the ground with a light groan. Your feet are tired, but you barely notice as you stare back up at the sky.

This great night is not so dark and terrible! How can it be when these beautiful lights exist to dance above you? Surely this is the perfect place to rest.

As you sit back and pull another dry ration from your bag, the bland taste does not even register.

There is something about the stars that is reminding you to have hope.

There are still no answers, but sitting there in the dark, your restless thoughts settle into an attentive openness. What does this great world have to show you?

I will admit Level Zero was just a taste, just a tutorial to the game you have entered now. By coming here, you have agreed to a journey. With warning, this journey is not easy or for the faint of heart. It will take time and dedication. It will take strength and courage.

So there is something to be said for starting by finding a little inspiration.

If you are a city dweller, perhaps you have never had the opportunity to see the stars expand above you in a million tiny lights, but if you have the opportunity, this is an experience you must make possible for yourself at some point in your life. I cannot truly put into words the sensations that bubbled up inside me when I first looked up at the stars without the light pollution of a city nearby. My mother and I had trekked from our home in the suburbs of Chicago out to the Grand Canyon National Park in Arizona. The national park is a certified dark skies park and an amazing place to see stars. It was a perfectly clear night. I saw all the stars for the first time that had always been hidden from me. Tiny balls of light, some even representing massive planets far off in our solar system. I felt completely humbled. I have since returned many times to re-experience this life-altering feeling.

Sitting below the dark expanse of night, you feel daunted, especially if you are a little afraid of the dark. You cannot see far beyond yourself. You don't know what's out there. However, when you tackle that fear and stare up, you are greeted with a surprise.

Staring up at the stars, it is easy to feel small and insignificant. If you flip that coin, it is also easy to feel the greatness of the universe expand before you. Such a great, massive world, and you are a part of it. You are living for just one tiny blip of the great expanse of time and space. Your problems, so giant to you, are just a drop of water in the chaos of time. But it's *your* blip of time. Just like the saying goes, "Dogs might be a small part of our lives, but to them we are their whole life," so, too, for you. You might be just a small story in the great story of time, but to you, it is the only story. I want your story to mean something—to you.

When you have been lost for a long time—lost in the to-do list, in the hustle, in the FOMO, in the should've would've could'ves of this world—you sometimes rush past the moments that will come to mean the most to you. Going even further, you tend to lose sight of how you can make more of those moments happen. When you are caught up in what you *ought* to do, without a strong center to hold you stable, you forget about what you *want* to do.

Now as we move forward, I am in no way saying that you should stop your life. It is impossible to uproot and abandon your present reality without causing a lot of backlash, both to yourself and to the people closest to you. So when I say we are fighting for our fairytale, this does not have to mean selling all your possessions and moving to a monastery in Nepal. Though if that's your fairytale, I truly hope you find a way to make it a reality. This does not mean abandoning your children and their needs to ride the waves of Hawaii all day every day.

This just means exploring the little ways, right here, right now, that you can take a step closer to the fairytale of the day, while keeping in mind the bigger fairytale of the future.

What you will come to find about fairytales is that, among the magic, there is normalcy. While soldiers are fighting Sauron at the gates of Mordor, there are hobbits back in the Shire planting gardens and teaching children (per the movies). Sometimes your life is going to look like the magic, and sometimes it is going to look like the normalcy. Both are part of your fairytale.

When I was going through all my cancer treatments, there was finally a week in August 2023, I remember it vividly, where I had no appointments to go to. That was a little fairytale I had been fighting toward for a very long time. A complete year in the making where I had been in a doctor's office every single week, and let me clue you in on a little secret, I'm terrified of needles of any kind. At the time, I worked remotely and did not have to run out in the middle of the afternoon to make an appointment. I just sat at home and worked nine to five. A little magical bit of normalcy.

Before that very special week, because I couldn't just NOT show up to my important treatments, marking another one off a physical calendar became a symbol of achievement to me each time I came home. I said it to myself quietly: I did it. I made it through another one. I am a step closer.

So know that I have your hand here. We are going to start small and easy when it comes to taking action. We may even just come to appreciate moments that happen outside of your control that are a blessing. Those first steps are going to help get the ball rolling. Once the ball is rolling, it is going to become easier and easier to take the bigger and harder actions that are going to make the bigger and more impactful changes in your life. So trust and take your time.

All the while, we are going to be keeping your normalcy in focus. Yes, we will still wash dishes or play with the kids or walk the dog. Or all of the above! Our normal life is going to become a part of the fairytale.

Before we move any further, I think it will be important to understand *how* to use this book. This book is laid out in two parts. Part One is where you find yourself now. This is where we begin the journey—on the inside. If your inside is not ready, if your mind is not prepared, no action that you take is going to get you any long-term results.

You are going to see things fall away and unravel, forgotten by the wayside before too long. So though the internal journey can be harder and downright boring sometimes—I know we cannot "see" the changes happening to us on the inside most of the time—know that by following the chapters and the activities one by one, you will have even greater success in Part Two.

Then, Part Two is where the action is going to kick in. We are going to choose your next adventure and dive head first into it. In your first read of this book, you will want to start with a small action, a side quest of sorts, like starting a new habit, breaking an old habit, working on a small project, or refocusing on something that makes you feel happy or fulfilled. We can call this the "everyday fairytale."

As you become more and more seasoned, these fairytales are going to start to evolve. Just like the characters in our favorite books only tackle the BBEG (big bad evil guy) after some other smaller successes, so, too, will you take on bigger challenges because your bigger fairytale is going to start to come into focus.

To give you a few examples that may or may not speak to you… maybe like me, you are going to write your own book! Or maybe you will pursue a new job or even a new career, apply to continuing education, move to a new city, adopt a pet, buy a home, save for a vacation, or a million other amazing achievements!

Your path is full of endless choices to make this fairytale your own.

Each chapter, or level, contains an actionable side quest. The side quests are small actions that you will implement to make progress on our guided adventure together. Most of these activities will be short and sweet, but as we progress they will get more and more involved, and more and more specific to your fairytale as you discover it. Eventually, you will leave my side quests behind in favor of your own true quest! How exciting!

At the end of each level, you will find a section I call "session recaps" where you will reflect on your progress through our adventure. Being the notetaker of the group is a really important job in RPG campaigns! This adventure reflection is often going to take the form of journaling. I know some of you are groaning and some are skipping around in glee! I know I have both in my camp here! Trust me on this, don't skip your adventure journaling session recaps, or else I am afraid this process might not work for you. Ever try to see something in the video game *Baldur's Gate 3* and fail your perception check? Yup, no good there. So, pass the checks and do your "homework."

If you don't enjoy journaling, or you want more guidance than a plain notebook, head to colleenochab.com/fairytalecompanionguide and download the FREE PDF companion guide that I created myself to help you follow along with this book. You can edit it online or print it out to carry along with you so you can feel the lovely pen in your hand as you write.

If you love journaling in a space of your own, now is the time to pull out your favorite notebook and pen. Flip the pages, try not to read your last entry, and place a special bookmark where you are going to begin to use your journal to fight for your fairytale. Or maybe, you can buy yourself a new, special notebook. Go ahead. Feed the guilty pleasure. Don't worry, we are quietly ignoring the ones that already sit barely used in a stack on a shelf.

Okay, have your Fight for Your Fairytale companion in hand? Great! It's time to explore a side quest and then sit down on your rock below the millions of stars and reflect.

SIDE QUEST:

If you are looking for inspiration, there is something uniquely special about taking a step out in nature that can get your creative juices flowing. For me, it is on walks through the woods that I have stumbled upon my very best plot ideas, especially if those woods are particularly dense and green, and I can imagine being a ranger in a dark cloak. It may seem like a no-brainer, but it took a walk through the woods on a refreshing morning for me to realize my bad guy deserved a redemption arc and an enemies-to-lovers plot. I think he will forever thank me for not leaving him in that dungeon to rot.

This is a great, big, beautiful world, and you are getting the opportunity to explore it. You! Just a tiny speck in the big picture. You, just a little existence amid the great forests, rivers, mountains, skies, stars, and universe.

So before you do anything else, please get up, put on your walking shoes, and take a lap outside. Leave your phone in your pocket and your ear buds out. If you live in the countryside, you probably don't have to go far to find yourself amid the open skies and greenery. If you live in the city, try to let your walk take you to a large park, somewhere where you can go into a little corner and forget about the hustle for a while. If you live near a body of water, go close to the edge of the shore.

As you walk away from home, first take time to notice what's around you. Can you hear the wind? Are there birds in the trees or squirrels running across the ground? Are other people's dogs barking? How does the air feel on your skin? Does it make you sticky with humidity? Or are you holding your arms tight in the snow? Can you see the sun's rays glinting through the leaves of the trees? Are the great trunks casting shadows across the ground?

Once you tune into your surroundings, let your gaze turn inward. At this moment, for five minutes, maybe ten, there is nothing else you need to do. When you go home, your to-do list will be waiting. But for now, it is okay to just be with yourself. Rest because rest is resistance. Tricia Hersey, a Black theologian, artist, and activist uses this phrase in her book, *Rest Is Resistance: A Manifesto*. She encourages individuals to reclaim their time and energy by prioritizing rest and reclaiming their divine right to rest. It is an act that can heal you from the daily grind and the challenge of the oppressive 'hustle culture' that prioritizes productivity over well-being.

So, check in with yourself. How are you feeling? What's on your mind? What thoughts are running through your head? Whatever comes, just let it be. There is nothing wrong here.

If you feel a sense of hope and anticipation, cling to that. If your mind drifts back to the TV show you watched last night, embrace it.

This walk is for you.

Often on my walks I step into the shoes of my character, Leona, and think through different imaginary situations. Maybe I know something is coming up in our campaign—how is she going to react? What is she going to do? Or sometimes I just pretend she is a part of other stories I am reading. How would she manage Valkyrie training with Nesta or fighting monsters with Geralt of Rivia?

So, if you haven't yet, set down this book and head out for a walk. I'll see you when you get back.

SESSION RECAP:

Welcome back, adventurer! How did that walk treat you? Be proud. You may have just completed your first walking meditation! Now is the time to open that companion guide if you have downloaded it from my website, or flip to the next clean page in your own journal.

You should be feeling pretty good after spending a little time out in nature. Perhaps you feel more relaxed or at peace. Maybe you feel energized. However you feel, tap into it. Let those positive energies flow out on the page.

This is an exercise that I have seen presented elsewhere, but I hope you will turn to look at it with new eyes. We are going to call this the "Wouldn't it be cool if…" list. The task is very simple. You will set a timer for ten minutes. For those ten minutes, you are going to write down every single thing that comes to mind that would be cool if it happened.

There are no good answers or bad answers. There are no smart answers or silly answers. Even things that are <u>impossible</u> would be cool if they happened.

So tap into your inner child. Tap into that adult who is staring up at the stars. If you gave yourself the capacity to dream again, if only to write it on this sheet of paper, what would you write?

I will give you a few examples that are very specific to me, just in case you need to get the creative juices flowing.

Wouldn't it be cool if…

- I got to play a character alongside the cast in an episode of *Critical Role* or *Worlds Beyond Number*

- I could purchase a giant farm and all my favorite pets (past/present/future) could come to live there together

- Some of my favorite celebrities starred in one of my movies: Ben Barnes, Lee Pace, Sam Hazeldine, or Kim Namjoon of BTS

- I could teleport wherever I needed to go instead of commuting there

- I am consistently making myself healthy meals

- I could purchase any gift I wanted for everyone on my list this Christmas

- I developed my fantasy books into a series of successful TV shows

The list goes on and on.

Set your timer for ten minutes and write as much as you can. It does not matter if it is impossible or really, really unlikely. It does not matter if it would be hard to make happen. All that matters is if you find it "cool." This is your inspiration time! Make it count.

As you finish your measly little dinner and lie with your head on your bag staring up at the stars, the desperation and hopelessness you felt for days seems to leak away into the night. Among the clusters of stars, you pick out images and animals. Some of the shapes you recognize as the constellations you were taught in school. Others, you know you are making up out of your own imagination.

It is fun to let your mind wander in this way. It almost feels like being a kid again. Opening your mind, you picture yourself flying on the back of a dragon, singing in a tavern, taking a tumble down a snow-covered hill far from home, opening your very own store, or just making a name for yourself amid all of the towns on the map.

Why can't it be true?

Why can't you try to become that adventurer?

Pursue those dreams, no matter how improbable?

That little flicker of hope that the stars gave you is growing.

As you lie there, drinking in the stars, staring up at the sky, and letting your eyes sweep across the horizon, you catch something. Your eyes are drawn to a distortion in the sky. You shake your head at first, but then you truly home in on it. A tendril of smoke is wafting up from somewhere in the forest. Not just a small tendril, a large one, like the smoke of many cook fires intertwining together.

There is a town nearby, or at least a camp. You don't know how long it will take you to reach that potential oasis, but now you know the direction to travel. You will find civilization, find direction at least, maybe within another day.

You blink once, twice.

What if it's not a town? What if you walk straight to a camp of bandits who steal all your possessions? Your mind starts to revert to old habits. The shadow of doubt and fear creeps back on your mind. You glance back into the forest. Is it really too late to turn back and go home?

Then, suddenly, you recognize that mean little voice in your head. You cannot drown it out, but you recognize it at least. This is anxiety and trepidation for the unknown.

Another day you can handle, and you will deal with the next challenge as it arises.

Despite battling a mental voice, you feel more settled than ever in the recent past, and find your heart more open and imaginative. You give yourself grace and take a deep breath. Yes, you are just going to take this journey one day at a time. You will fear the bandit camp tomorrow.

You cradle your head and fall asleep.

What Holds Us Back & Propels Us Forward

"You are carrying too much to be able to run."

From every quest in Bethesda's Skyrim ever

The next morning comes cold but glorious, even the looming threat of a bandit camp doesn't completely dampen the spirit you feel looking out upon the nature before you. Outside of the tree line, you are able to watch as the sunrise peeks up from beyond the mountains far away on the horizon. You see the rays glitter off the snow-covered peaks. You have never climbed a mountain peak, but maybe one day soon you will get the chance to try.

The warm yellow rays touch your face, and slowly you stand and shake off the evening chill. Your eyes blink through the sleep in the coming daylight. As you look out, the world seems different. The sky is a patchwork of silver, purple, pink, blue, and gold. Even the trees look different. Though they surround you like a great ocean of green, you take in the patterns and colors. Bluish-green in a strip there, a brush of purple amid a circle of forest green. Everywhere you look are different colors and textures.

Now, since you know where to look, you stare across the tree line to the smoky distortion in the sky. Yes, there is definitely some sort of civilization there. A clearing amid all the trees. Maybe it is a bandit camp or maybe a town, but you know you only have a day's journey to get there. Or maybe two.

You set to work gathering your things. You take a few minutes just to bask in the sunlight and soak in the sights up here on this rocky outcropping. If you are right, there is at least another day of travel in the dark woods, so you have to make the most of this sunlight. When you have eaten a little breakfast and finally hefted your bag on your back, you begin your careful climb back down the boulders into the forest.

The rocks you climbed in your pursuit of the light last night were indeed quite steep. Going the other direction, you have trouble finding the hand and foot holds you used before. Luckily, there are plenty of vines, dead and alive, covering the rocks as you slip down among the boughs of the trees. You test them as you go, making sure none are going to pull out when you place your full weight on them.

You are halfway down when you pick the wrong handhold. It wouldn't be a problem, except the large pack on your back has changed your normal center of gravity. Your upper body shifts backward away from the rock, and your hands scramble and scratch in front of you, clinging and grasping at vines, praying they will catch you. Gravity's strength, however, is beyond your own.

You fall backward ten feet to the next boulder. It catches you unceremoniously by your back, shoving your pack into your body.

You hear the *whoosh* as the air escapes your lungs. Coughing, you turn onto your side and then push yourself up to your hands and knees. It could have been worse. It could have been way worse.

The last boulder is barely five feet from the forest floor, so you scooch forward on your butt and slide the rest of the way down. The vines make it a bumpy ride and your pack catches a little halfway through, but then you find yourself back on level ground.

Standing up and brushing dirt from your clothes, you let your eyes readjust to the darkness within the forest. Now that the sun is back up, there is enough light to see by. You cannot see the rays, but they reach you, heavily filtered through the leaves.

You find yourself whistling a tune as you search your way back to the little game trail and head in the direction of those tendrils of smoke. You know you cannot see them now, but you have a general sense of the direction you need to go. You carefully remind yourself to check your surroundings with your nose as well. It might be able to aid and guide you there.

The first few hours of your day pass without issue, but as the midday nears, you find yourself rolling your neck. It feels very stiff, and your lower back has been aching with pain for days. This blasted pack. If only you didn't need to carry everything you needed to survive constantly along with you.

You pull at the straps and try to lower it, but by lowering the pack, your little bedroll swings and smacks your butt each time you take a step. Growling, you try to heft it higher on your back, but it doesn't sit naturally there, and you have to hold a constant grip on your straps with your hands to make sure it doesn't slide back down.

As the true midday rolls around, your sweat pools and gathers in the heat. This. This is the final straw. This pack has to go. At least for a little while.

The physical discomfort triggers your pessimism.

Your mind spirals off again like it did last night. Why can't they make better, more comfortable packs? Isn't there magic you could learn to make your pack hover alongside you instead of physically putting in the effort? Why did no one teach you something as useful as that?

You find a little creek and drop to the ground beside it, tossing your pack off your shoulders and to the side. As you drink quietly from the water, you kick your pack for good measure.

You are so close, so close to civilization, but now you are feeling drained and held back by this dumb item on your back. You know you need it. You made a list and packed everything so carefully until it was near bursting, everything for your adventure. Honestly, it wasn't even everything you needed. It was hard to leave that second waterskin at home because you could have used it, but there just was no room left to put it.

As you cool off physically beside the creek, your mental voice calms and quiets as well. You listen to the water and let it recenter you. There has to be *something* you can do to make the journey a little easier.

You open your bag and shake out its contents onto the ground. There has to be something you can leave behind. This bag is too damn heavy for you to keep going. You need to be light and nimble on your feet so you can get to that oasis of civilization as soon as possible. However, as you rummage through, it is hard to make any decision.

You need those things like the clothes on your back, the bedroll tied to the outside, and the rations and waterskin. All the things you need to survive. The little dagger on your belt is necessary for protection. Your money pouch is all that you have to your name. Obviously you cannot part with your hairbrush and hand mirror. Once you get to town, you will be happy to be able to clean yourself up and look presentable again. Otherwise you are going to look like a fool. The townspeople are going to think you are some traveling vagabond.

You have a map of the world. You have to keep that! How else are you going to know where all the continents are? Even if the map shows little of the terrain or the smaller towns, you have to know that the capital city is along the coast several hundred leagues away. When a lost traveler comes up to you asking for directions, it is going to be really helpful to set them back on their way again, and you will look like an expert!

Deeper in your pack, you have a few things you especially cannot part with. There is the golden, gem-encrusted music box. Not only is it worth more than a pretty penny, but it was your great aunt's best friend's music box. It plays a little tune that your family said was her favorite, even though you have never met her to know any better. Beside it sits a book your best friend gave to you when you were kids. They found it in the middle of the street, so it's a bit worn and has mud stains all over it. You know some of the pages are missing, ripped out, and you never tried to read the whole thing, but it reminds you of them. You could never bear to part with it.

There is the little whittled piece of wood that your first love made for you. They took the chunk from the tree out in the backyard after it was struck by lightning. Besides the whittling marks they made and your carved initials, you can still see the burn marks. It smells like a campfire. You wonder what they are doing now. You never even saw them again after the end of your relationship years ago.

On and on your items go, and slowly you begin to realize how few of them are actually necessary now that you are in the dark wood. True, a lot of them are memories, but you could have left them back home in the room your guardians still keep open and available to you, or maybe you could have written about them in your journal instead of keeping them and lugging them around.

That's where they would better serve you, in your mind as memories, rather than holding you back from reaching the end of this wood. Mercilessly, you start tossing items aside. Yes, starting with that wood chip from a relationship that you wouldn't even want anymore. With each item you set aside, you feel a little shred of pessimism lift from your mind, like the physical items removed from your pack are also removing the mental items from your past.

I am in that portion of my life where I am always moving. First, it was back and forth to college for four years of undergrad. It is always amazing how much stuff you can pack in a tiny dorm room, no? I am sure the parents of daughters feel me in that experience. Then, it was back and forth between living with my parents and moving to a house with post-college roommates. Then, back to the parents' during chemo. Now, my first apartment with my partner. I know I still have many moves ahead as we look to buy our first house.

Even if you haven't moved physically in recent years, I am sure you have gone on a trip where you have packed too much. This is especially easy when you are traveling by car instead of flying. At least those airline weight restrictions hold us back most of the time. Though

I have paid my share of airport baggage fees, especially outside of the United States.

When my mom and I took our road trip to the Grand Canyon with our rescue dog, I vividly remember lugging his crate back and forth from the car as we stopped at vacation rental houses each night. Call him spoiled, but Nod loves to sleep in his crate at night, and he had to travel in it in the car for his safety. So big sissy to the rescue carrying it wherever he needed it day and night!

Yet, sometimes, unlike Nod's crate, which he used ceaselessly throughout that trip, we discover a number of things that we packed that we never even used. Yes, I am talking about that fancy outfit for the dinner out you decided not to go to or the sunhat you swore you were going to wear at the beach, but you got a sunburn on your face anyway.

We often overpack for fear of the unknown. If you are a planner, you try to prepare for every possible scenario. In your daily life, however, planning endlessly for the unexpected is exhausting and stressful.

When we are away from home, those items we packed can be that normalcy and connection to home that we crave, but they can also be a heavy weight we sweat with as we carry a heavy rolling suitcase up a staircase in a beautiful, but cobblestoned, seaside town.

Okay, enough with the analogies. If we take a step back, we know that this can apply to our life in many ways. Our baggage presents itself in different places and capacities. When you are lost, you need to learn to let go of the things that are holding you back from discovering and pursuing your fairytale. You need to embrace the things that you are ignoring that might be guiding you closer.

For a long time in my life, I lived with a lot of fear. To the outside world, no one would have ever guessed. Especially in my work situations, I moved forward with confidence and skill, a lot of things came naturally for me, and I could pick up on new tasks quite easily. But as you know, I avoided exploring writing for a career. Instead, I danced around my interest out of fear. I didn't know how to become a published author or a screenwriter. My family had no background in entertainment and that kind of work. How could I possibly do that? I avoided it because of my fear of failure. I had to maintain my long run of success.

When chemo literally forced me to sit back and unpack it all, when life appeared to shorten before my eyes, that morbid inspiration helped me drop the fear for the first time ever. With new inspiration and Leona holding my hand (even though she loathes holding hands), I moved forward.

Because what my fear was not letting me see was that it did not matter if I didn't know how to become a writer and screenwriter. Someone out there in the world did! There are thousands, if not millions, of writers in the world, especially throughout history. If they could do it, so could I. If I was smart enough to research a paper for school, I could research and find the resources to pursue my own dream.

That's when it clicked. That baggage of fear dropped away for me. Feeling lighter than ever before, drastic action became possible, even fighting through tears.

They say when one door closes, another door opens. This could be true of a job, a loss of a pet or a partner, a tragic accident, or even trauma. Now, not all baggage is created equal, and some are much harder to drop than others, but the recognition of your baggage is the first step to releasing its load on you.

After my cancer journey, I had to come to terms with my new body that was not capable of the same things it once was. Due to my double mastectomy, I will never breastfeed my children if I am able to have them. In some ways, I started to feel incomplete and broken—like my body wasn't capable of doing what it should be. Sometimes that threatened to break my heart. On the other hand, I also had the chance to choose the way I wanted my chest to look during my reconstruction, something a lot of other women dream about being able to do.

After my car accident the following year, I lost a car that had been gifted to me by my uncle when he passed away. I missed the freedom of having my own vehicle and the financial security of not having a regular car payment. I missed the memory of my uncle that the car would inspire. However, sharing a car for a time helped my partner and I become closer in our relationship and practice good communication skills—something I am glad we did *before* we got engaged.

A few months later, my father had a heart attack on my birthday and died a few days later in the ICU. It was hard on my mother and I, but in the end, he was no longer in pain, and I believe his last day was a good one.

Sometimes life is unreal. Cancer, car accident, loss of a parent? All in a span of less than two years? I could go on and on with the reflections I have done into these heavy loads in my life. There were MANY times I wanted to say "screw it" and throw in the towel. I wanted to bemoan life and all the negative problems it was throwing my way all at once. When you are going through the thick of a storm, you likely don't see any of the good yet. It probably has not found its way to you, but know that it's there.

That December after my father's loss passed by in a blur—planning and attending the funeral, healing from my reconstruction surgery. The weather was cold and dreary. The storm wasn't just outside on the roads, it was within. So, I allowed myself to be sad amid cozy blankets and twinkling Christmas lights. We stayed in and had a quiet Christmas. Our doggos were intense sources of comfort. Sometimes that's all you can do, sit together quietly through the pain. In the quiet moments when I was alone physically, Leona still sat beside me. She understood the pain and grief I was feeling, and sometimes just having someone who can say "Hey, I've been there" is all you need.

I won't say any of these are a trauma I have completely dealt with. I don't think I want to ever forget about them because they have crafted who I am today. I have, however, packed them into light, easy to carry items that I can pull out and remember every once in a while. I carry them with me, but they don't provide a burden to my load.

If you are fighting trauma, I am not saying you should be happy for your trauma because it made you stronger or more resilient. You did not deserve to have that horrible thing happen to you. I am sorry you had to get stronger in that way. I hope you can recognize your baggage and seek to lighten its load on you. For as you move forward with life, you deserve to be able to fight for your fairytale. You deserve to move beyond whatever trauma lurks in the shadows of your past. Despite its significance, I hope you grow beyond it through the coming pages, because you are so much more than your trauma or your past.

If you need some inspiration as we move into the side quest and session recap portion of this chapter, just think of Frodo carrying the Ring to Mordor. Frodo was the only one who could bear it. Not Aragorn, not Gandalf, not any number of strong, wonderful characters that present themselves throughout the story. No, it was Frodo and Sam who could carry the Ring of Power. It was a trauma given to them that they did not ask for. They did not want that burden. It almost destroyed them on several occasions. When the movies end and the Ring is gone, you know that the baggage of carrying the Ring has not left them.

However, both Frodo and Sam move beyond the Ring. They return home, though nothing feels the same. They manage their trauma. Frodo sails to the Undying Lands, another adventure. Sam marries the love of his life and has beautiful children. The next part of their fairytales happen, even with the baggage of their past that they carry. Their fairytales continue regardless of what transpired before.

So, too, can you acknowledge your current inventory and lighten the burden. Sometimes it is in looking at it, saying hello, and letting it truly exist that we can reduce the power of those burdens on us. Sometimes it lets us truly realize how much our extra luggage is holding us back. Maybe we realize we cannot face it or fight it alone. Maybe we ask for the help of a friend or a therapist to help us fight the dark shadows.

So let's dump that pack on the floor and shuffle through the contents. With respect and love, let's explore those things that might be holding you back from fighting for your fairytale with all your might. You may be surprised what you find along the way that will propel you into your future adventure!

SIDE QUEST:

Sometimes to clear out the mind it helps to clear out the physical space first. For those who are going through a difficult depression, this may be exactly what you physically don't feel up to doing, so I am going to give you a variety of options here to meet you where you are at in this moment.

My best friend made an observation of me while we lived together in college that "the cleanliness of my room was directly proportional to the cleanliness of my mind." And no, she did not mean the romance books. When I was stressed about school, or a big test, or a project, the organization in my room faltered. I would leave things cluttered everywhere, including dirty dishes! Don't do that to your roomies! When I cleaned my room, even when the school stresses still existed, I found I could manage them much easier.

It was in learning that reality about myself that I became a better roommate and partner. Today, I still tend to get messy when I am upset, busy, or stressed, but I do keep my home in much better order. For my partner, this significantly impacts his happiness and it makes our home a better place.

So before you move on and start weed-whacking the jungle of your mind, let's first turn to something a little more tangible.

What is one space in your home—whether your bedroom, office, bathroom, kitchen, basement, storage space, etc.—where there is a mess you keep saying you will get to? You know you need to clean it up or organize it, but you don't. So it lingers like a weight in the back of your mind. Yup, that thing you just thought of is baggage too.

If you have the time now, set aside this book and go do that thing. If it is something you need to leave for tomorrow, maybe it's 2 am and you really can't start vacuuming and wake up everyone in the house, bookmark this section and don't move on until you have done that one little thing.

Let me clarify now. One little mess!

Clear the clutter from your kitchen counter. Dust off your desk. Clean a single toilet. Don't make this a huge project that is going to overwhelm you after ten minutes.

If cleaning, organizing, or sorting physically doesn't sound good to you right now, instead declutter your mind by creating a little list of things you want to organize or clean in the future.

Insert the *Jeopardy!* waiting music here. Off to work you go!

Now that you're back and your little mess has been cleared, how do you feel? I know it might be something seemingly small and insignificant, but you just lightened your load. Now that you know what it feels like, it is going to become easier and easier to lighten the load in different and even more substantial ways.

If this little activity felt REALLY good, make note of this book for later. Check out *The Life Changing Magic of Tidying Up* by Marie Kondo when you have finished my book. I am winking at you. They also made it a Netflix show, but I insist the book is better. There is even an illustrated, comic book version for those who enjoy that!

Marie speaks of the methods to tidying up your space and filling your space with the things that spark joy. I can't imagine a better place to start fighting for your fairytale than making your space the place you WANT to live in, no matter how small. Make your home feel right and you are a step closer to your fairytale. Stick that in your mind for later. You might want to return to this.

SESSION RECAP:

Now we are back to our companion guide or journal. If you are in the zone of tidying, I know you may want to keep going, keep cleaning; however, we need some quiet time to turn inward. So, first make a to-do list of all the things that clutter the back of your mind that you know you need to get to, but keep putting off. Just putting them down on paper is going to do wonders for you. It is going to release all that mental space you were using to remember your to-do list to start dreaming up your fairytale.

Once you have done that, let's start digging a little deeper. Let's explore these questions. Open up your journal so you have two pages facing you.

1. On the left-hand sheet of paper: What do you feel is holding you back? Is it something mental like fear, insecurity, or confusion? Or is it something physical like your finances, your health, where you live, etc.? Write down anything that comes to mind. Try not to label right or wrong. We will craft plans later in Part Two of this book.

2. On the right-hand sheet of paper: What is something that always makes you feel inspired? If you work during the week, how are you filling your evenings or weekends when you are the happiest? What do you genuinely enjoy doing? If you're struggling with finding inspiration right now, what is something you've always wanted to do, or what's something that inspired you as a child?

Once you have journaled this, sit back. Look at the paper before you from a distance. Think of the words before you like a scale. Are there more items listed on the left or the right hand sheet of paper? This will tell you which way your mental state is skewing. Were you able to think of more baggage? Or was your mind busy exploring inspiration?

Whatever your result, this is just a starting point. No matter where you start, this is the journey of this book: to reconnect with your inspiration, uncover your strengths, come to peace with areas where you struggle, and break free of the chains holding you back.

Let's start adding to the side of inspiration.

Is there any way that you could start doing more inspiring things in your life right now to keep your mental state skewing toward being a problem-solving explorer? Look back at your "Wouldn't it be cool if…" list and circle all of the things that you feel might be possible for you to start doing more of right now. You don't have to actually take action at this moment, just circle it in your journal. I might circle "I am consistently making myself healthy meals." That's something I could try to do that would make me happy *and* healthy!

In your list, you might not find a direct transition to an action you can take, but look for a pattern or commonalities between what you have listed. What is the core goal of some of your "cool" ideas? This might lead you toward little inspiring things you are able to do right now.

Once you have circled all the possibilities, add two or three more items to the right side of your paper. Slowly, inspiration for rediscovering your fairytale grows.

You hesitate, even as you toss the precious golden music box to the side, with that book from your best friend in your hands. You have never read it. You have never thought much of it, but you realize it means a lot to you. It reminds you of their friendship. It is a friendship that does not cease over distance or time. Even if you are separated, you know you will pick up right where you left off when you come together again. Yes, though you have unloaded several pounds of unnecessary junk, this muddy, old book is staying tucked in your bag.

As you carefully reassemble your pack with all the things you plan to keep with you on your journey, your hands squeeze the flint and steel. You put it back in your pack even as you frown. It is necessary for survival if you are any good at making a fire. What is the point in carrying it though if you do not have the skill to build a life-saving fire with it?

No, no, it does not matter. It's hot. It's the middle of the day. No fire needed. You have gotten along just fine without a fire for days, especially when you had the stars. Perhaps you'll get along just fine forever.

LEVEL THREE - DEFICIENCIES

Grow or Discard What's Complicated

"Once you've accepted your flaws, no one can use them against you."

FROM TYRION LANNISTER IN GEORGE
R.R. MARTIN'S A GAME OF THRONES

*Author's note: Before moving further in this chapter, I want to acknowledge the negative connotation that revolves around the word "deficient" when attached to people. In no way am I saying one is "deficient," "not good enough," or "lacking" by not having a particular skill. In RPG games, proficiencies are typically special skills or abilities your character possesses that give them advantages in particular situations. While the opposite is not particularly called deficiencies, not having a certain skill tends to put your character at a disadvantage when trying to take an action utilizing that skill, ultimately making it harder to achieve. We will treat our deficiencies here in the same way. These are skills we may not yet have, or perhaps even skills we never wish to pursue developing. Acknowledging them will ultimately be what's most important.

As your trek continues, the forest takes on the heat of the height of the day. Now that your pack is lighter, you don't feel like you are being dragged to the earth, but your feet still hurt and you can feel the sweat soaking through your shirt, especially on your back beneath your pack. You tear off your cloak and scrunch it in a ball alongside your bedroll.

There were a lot of things you did not think about when it came to adventuring. Throwing your dagger, no problem. You probably could even maneuver a sword pretty well if asked to. That's what adventurers do, right? They fight monsters and bad guys while they travel across the world taking in the sights.

However, you forgot about all the other "smaller" things that adventurers have to deal with. Like spiders. You really hate the feel of spiders' webs on your skin, and recently it feels like you get a faceful every couple of minutes. At first, you swung your arms and blustered and stomped as the shivers ran through your body, but now you just peel the little strings away from your skin. You're glad you haven't gotten any live spiders on you though. That you still wouldn't be able to tolerate.

You could list the endless supply of other things you forgot adventurers have to tolerate. There are the cold nights and hot days. The uncomfortable, rocky sleeping arrangements. The ceaseless bland rations because you are not really one to hunt. The emptiness of the road. The endless anxiety of the night when you're alone with no one to stand guard. You really don't sleep the best, because every sound startles you awake.

Amazing the amount of normal, boring things you have to put up with when you set out on an adventure.

That's why they skip over the "boring parts" in books. The tales would be rather dull if you had to stop with your hero every time they had to relieve themselves. Speaking of, you should probably do that right now.

Luckily, the day continues without much of the unexpected. You continue on, and the faint smell of smoke grows. Maybe you are just hopeful. Maybe you are just imagining it, because the light begins to lessen again. The sunset is here. You have not reached whatever town or camp you might have seen from a distance last night.

Stepping a few paces off the trail, you find a tiny clearing and begin to move away the broken sticks and rocks. You make a nice, clear space for yourself. As you roll out your bedroll and settle down, your space grows darker. You stare at that pile of sticks that you gathered. Is it worth it? Should you try to build a fire?

Old you would have said no. There is too much evidence from nights previous that you are incapable of building a fire. You're tired. You're frustrated. You're hungry. You desperately want a bath. It would be so much easier to just lie down, curl up, and go to bed, defeated again.

However, there is a new you awakening. The spark of hope that you'll be out of the woods soon is kindling an ember of a fire that now burns brighter than it has in quite some time.

The new voice that you are slowly getting used to says to give it just one more try.

You set some stones in a little circle a few feet away from your bedroll and then hunt for a few larger branches. Some narrow logs catch your eye, but you are not looking to build a bonfire. Just a little crackling thing to warm your space.

Returning with a few branches of a thin diameter, you carefully arrange them as you have seen the workers at the inn do in the past. You rack your brain. What did they always say? You have to let the fire breathe.

Filling the space in the middle lightly with smaller twigs and some leaves, you pull out your flint and steel. You angle it carefully toward your stack of leaves.

Snap. Strike. You try to craft the spark.

But nothing. You were too hesitant.

Snap. Strike. A little bit harder.

A little ember shoots forward but doesn't reach your leaves. You take a breath.

Snap. Strike.

This time your little flame dances to the leaves. The thin leaf catches fire and burns. You watch as the flame spreads. You are so pleased.

Then the miniature wall of flame disintegrates before your eyes.

The hope in your chest drops into your stomach. You snatch what's left of the leaf. Molding and wet. Suddenly you notice many of the twigs and sticks are moist, too. This is going to be a lot more difficult than you even originally thought.

There is a quote that I love from Cleanthes that says, "The fates guide the person who accepts them, and hinder the person who resists them." I think about that quote a lot. It inspires both Level Three and

Level Four of our journey. So while we might discuss the hindrances here, hold out hope that our guides will return to us next. I promise.

I want to make a disclaimer as well that this chapter is not telling you to give up on a dream because you are not yet good at it, are afraid of failing at it, or think you aren't cut out for it. That is a very different topic. Frankly, one I do not endorse.

Acknowledging our deficiencies is about setting aside our own expectations. It is about making realizations that perhaps you really don't want the things the world might say you should want, or even the things *you* wanted long ago. This is about discovering an honest piece of yourself, even if it ends up being a challenging flaw.

Our flaws are as much a part of who we are as the strengths we boast. Though, just like our baggage, our deficiencies—shortcomings, imperfections, flaws, failures—could be what's holding us back. For Leona, one of her flaws is that she has no charisma. Speaking to people is really hard for her. Convincing people in an argument is even harder. That's why she, unfortunately, solves many problems with her fists and not her voice. It takes other people taking the lead in those situations for her to succeed, and once she came to terms with that, our party moved along A LOT more easily.

Luckily, just like our inventory, we have the capacity to turn the tables on our deficiencies. The challenge is to discover the best way to turn the tables in the right direction, and it's going to look different for everyone. Only you can choose the way to go.

So why do these deficiencies exist? In the case of our conversation, the deficiencies appear when we may lack the skills in an area that we need to be skilled in. Yet, we consistently put learning that skill on the back burner for other "easier" things. We prioritize instant gratification over things we know we want because it's just that—more gratifying. In such a fast-paced, go-go-go world, we've forgotten the art of patience and long-term dedication.

This is the child learning how to ride a bike without training wheels who decides they'd rather not try again because they fell off yesterday. This is the person who avoids going back to school because they have to focus on finding a better job, when school would lead to a better job. This is the writer who should be working on mastering their writing craft, but consistently goes back to the latest book they were reading or to scrolling social media instead. Don't worry! I'm calling myself out here with *that* example!

These sorts of deficiencies are easy to note and yet harder to accept.

It is normal, in fact, it's almost an expectation, that most things in life we will not be good at. Not at the beginning. Not while we are learning. If you've ever heard of the 10,000-hour rule based on the research of Anders Ericsson, who studied expert musicians and found that those who had practiced for approximately 10,000 hours tended to be more skilled than those who had practiced for less time, you know the biggest skills are developed over years of carefully sculpted practice. When fighting for the fairytale, knowing your fairytale is going to give you a map. Then, you will decide where to dedicate your 10,000 hours. There's going to be a lot of work needed, but if you really care about your fairytale, you are going to find a way to make it a reality. You craft your fairytale each time you wake up. Step by step.

Our deficiencies may be skills that we work at and develop over time on the road to reaching our fairytale, but alternatively, it might be acknowledging where you just need some extra help. Where can you be honest with yourself and admit you are holding yourself back?

An example might be learning how to use a computer. If you need it for school or your job, it would probably be worthwhile to take some extra lessons or courses to practice and get more familiar so it's a skill that doesn't hold you back. Alternatively, if you are a farmer who doesn't need a computer, you may just outsource when it comes time to worry about a website, marketing, or even sending emails!

I played volleyball for years at a very competitive level. I trained and trained and trained. Hours every week dedicated to this sport. For me, all the years put in were never enough to play first string on the college team. In those final years, I could have let that hold me back. I could have gotten down on myself for not being good enough. Instead, it was time for a shift in perspective. I started being honest with myself, and finally giving volleyball up allowed for new passions to bloom. Frankly, these new passions were things I could ultimately become a professional at. And man, being proficient (a RPG term for being super skilled) feels good, but I digress.

If you have a limitation, a physical or mental disability—your situation is much different than the struggle to attain a skill. If you are differently abled, you do not need to be fixed or "get better." You might not have the opportunity to be great at certain things. Every body has its limits, but you do have incredible opportunities with other skills, maybe skills or passions you haven't even discovered yet.

So, if you are someone who identifies as being differently abled, you may not have the choice of what you face, but you do have the choice of your perspective. We all can learn from you. Commit to crafting a world that makes your dreams possible, just as you are. That's part of your calling.

In this book, we are learning how to fight for our own fairytale. That means stepping up to be the creator. To be the creator is to take responsibility and authority in the journey. And so, how we choose to manage our deficiencies is integral to our success.

Now is the particular time in our journey to consider if what we struggle with is worth putting our time and energy into improving, or if we should acknowledge it and move on to something else. This is where you decide which route you personally are going to take. Does this mean discarding it completely? Not necessarily. It may, if that's what you decide, or you could reimagine it: take a different path to the same goal or find a sidekick (the Sam to your Frodo) to balance your skillset.

SESSION RECAP:

We are doing this a little backward in this chapter, because it will behoove you to have some reflection here before you take some action. This is one of my favorite exercises that I have explored on this journey. Turn to your companion guide or open up your notebook.

Now we are going to split our page in two. Draw a big line down the middle.

Ruminate first on these questions:

- Who do you look up to?

- Who do you wish you could be more like?

- Who is doing something you wish you could be doing right now?

- Who inspires you or lives the life you would like to live?

Think of your favorite characters. They don't have to be from a fantasy novel. They could come from any story or movie. They could be your player character in a campaign. They could even come from the real world. Do not limit yourself here.

Now, jot their names down on the left side of your paper and leave a bit of room below each one.

You already know that I look up to my RPG character, Mereoleona. I might also add other fictional characters I love to that list, like Belle from *Beauty and the Beast* or Elizabeth Swan from *Pirates of the Caribbean*. Some of my friends might name Taylor Swift to their list or even their professor who has inspired them to pursue their career path.

These names are important because these are the characters who are going to walk with you until you are ready to fly on your own. Their stories, their fairytales, will be what we use to catch a glimpse into what we are missing in our own lives. It is how we will start to explore ourselves.

Underneath each of these names, I want you to brainstorm.

- Did anything hold these people or characters back?

- What hardships did they face?

- What difficulties did they confront?

These can be both internal or external challenges. Write all that comes to mind down on the left side of the paper under each of their names.

For example, I might say Belle faced living with the Beast, feeling like an outsider among the townspeople, having to fight off or ignore the advances of Gaston, being trapped in a small town unable to go out and adventure because of her duty to her aging father, etc. For Elizabeth, her list might be living up to the expectations of her father, acting like a noble English lady, fighting for survival against ghost pirates, and choosing the real love of her life.

Some of these are internal, some are external. Both are good to notice. The more you can home in on those internal, mental limitations—the easier this will get.

Now that you have journaled this, sit back. Look at the words before you. Is there anything similar between the challenges your inspirational characters or people faced and what you face right now? You probably will be able to draw a few comparisons. Let that soak in.

When you are ready, in the right-hand column, write what you have in common with your comfort characters or people. Maybe you share a hardship. Maybe you both can't hold your tongue. Or maybe, your experiences are quite different, but you realize that they, too, have faced struggles all their own. Whatever the result, note it there beside the name in the right column.

I think you will discover hardships and flaws are what make us human. These characters are just like us, living in different worlds. Welcome them into your company. They are going to travel with you from here on out.

SIDE QUEST:

Now that we have gathered our supportive crew, it is time to put in some action. For catharsis, this is going to be really simple, because dealing with our flaws and deficiencies can be heavy as hell. If you enjoy meditation or yoga, this is a great opportunity to settle into your body, settle into your mind, and work on release. I love letting go and letting my body sink into the floor in child's pose.

For lots of people, meditation or yoga just gets the mind racing. Am I breathing right? Is my body in the right shape? So, as an alternative, we are going to release these tensions in a different way.

If you have access to a bunch of tennis balls and a safe space to throw them, get to gathering. Or, if you need to stay in one place, get a bunch of sticky notes or small strips of paper.

You can write your difficulties, deficiencies, flaws, and hardships directly on the tennis balls and sticky notes, or you can just imagine what they represent in your head. Think carefully. Once you've done that—CHUCK THEM! Yes, throw them! One by one.

If you are using tennis balls, head out to the court and throw them or hit them with as much power as you can. Let out your tennis scream. If you have the stickies, fold them up and flick them like that paper football thing everyone did in middle school in the early 2000s. Get that release!

We choose to let go what we are capable of letting go and face what we need to face. We are people who do what we gotta do. We are making the fairytale happen. We are fighting the fight. We will live to see another, better day.

Another day draws to a close, and you lie there in the dark beside the skeleton of the fire you failed to craft. On other nights, the thought might have kept you awake, the thought of failure. You lie back and stare at the overhanging tree boughs. Tonight, you hear the negative thoughts, but they're quieter. You can debate with them now rather than sulk in their assumed truth.

Yes, you were never any good at crafting a fire. Perhaps it is something you can learn, find someone to teach you. But for now, you can let it be.

Thinking of the world and how big it is, there are probably one hundred thousand things you don't know how to do or are downright terrible at. Tonight, that doesn't bother you one bit. In fact, it excites you. Think of how many things, wonderful things, that are out there in the world just waiting to be learned.

So you close your eyes, and instead your brain reminds you that there are plenty of skills you do have. It is not your fault you just haven't needed them trekking through the deep woods.

LEVEL FOUR - PROFICIENCIES

Lean Into What Comes Naturally

*"A sword wields no strength unless the
hand that holds it has courage."*

From Hero's Shade in Nintendo's Legend
of Zelda: The Twilight Princess

*Author's note: In RPG games, proficiencies are typically special skills or abilities your character possesses that give them advantages in particular situations. In the *Dungeons and Dragons 5e* version, for example, D&D Beyond shares, "If you have proficiency with something, you can add your Proficiency Bonus to any d20 roll you make using that thing. A creature might have proficiency in a skill or saving throw or with a weapon or tool." This idea means that taking an action you have a skill in makes it vastly easier to accomplish than if you didn't.

Despite rising with sore bones the following morning, you toss a quick glance at your sad little fire pit and its moldy leaves and laugh.

Quickly, with the light growing, you start making your way again. It may just be a trick of the eye, but you almost swear the trees are thinning.

The day continues on without event, and slowly sunset approaches.

You catch a whiff of a delightful smoke. This time your mouth waters because you can clearly note the tang of meat in the air. The scent is so strong. It is like nothing you have smelled in over a week. Your feet move of their own accord. Your nose guides the way. You barely notice where you are headed.

In the dark forest, you can see visions of chicken and mutton. Some greasy piece of delicious meat turns on a spit over the fire. Faster and faster your feet drive you.

The light is growing again, like it did when you climbed the rocks and saw the stars. You are greeted by an opening in the trees ahead after turning another curve. Stepping on, you plunge through the end of the tree line. Suddenly you realize you have been nearly flying down a hill. You have finally reached the bottom of the mountain pass.

Your eyes are drawn to the distortion in the sky, which you quickly realize is a tendril of smoke wafting up from the chimney of an inn, nestled securely in the middle of a tiny village, in the middle of a happy-looking valley, in the middle of the great mountains.

No bandit camp. An actual village.

A grateful respite on the long road.

Safety. Security.

You may be nowhere near the end of your journey, but you have made it through this forest, appearing at a friendly wayside where you can stop and rest and refresh before stepping out on the road again.

A sheep bleats at you loudly. It shocks you as you look down and see the creature at your right, peering up at you closely. Your laugh is hearty as you tap it lightly on the head.

Good to see you, too!

You adjust your pack and begin the last bit of the trek over the fields into the village. Carefully you dust off your clothes, suddenly self-conscious, but surely this little tucked-away village has seen a rugged traveler or two before. You hurry down the path toward the town. Soon, your little trail connects with a wide open road. You pass a farmer heading out of town with a donkey and a cart. He dips his head in greeting as you pass.

You gutter out a hello. You are shocked by the sound of your unused voice; however, he doesn't seem to mind or think anything of it.

Suddenly the little homes and storefronts are all around you. This is a simple village, but clearly enough of a stopping point along the road to do good business. There is a bakery and a blacksmith. There is an apothecary, and yes, a tavern in the town square connected to a leaning, three-story inn.

Your tired feet drive you there as the sunset blooms overhead. As you push the door open, a cheerful din meets your ears. You step past some crowded tables. A few patrons glance at you, but no one pays you much mind. Suddenly, you find yourself eye to eye with the barkeep.

He gives you a look over before speaking in a deep and rolling voice. "Welcome traveler. You have seen your time on the road."

"Yes," you say. "I am looking to purchase a room."

"That'll be three silver."

You consider. In a place like this, it's probably a little high. Though, you have not yet seen the state of the rooms.

You always were decent at haggling though.

"I'll give you seven silver up front for three nights," you say carefully. "And you'll throw in meals."

He glances at you, surprised. A few other patrons sitting along the bar look without hiding it. The barkeep notices this as well. You keep your gaze determined on the man before you. "Nine silver," he says. "And aye, I'll throw in breakfast and dinner each day."

You don't glance toward the other patrons, though you wish you could study them. You cannot tell if the other patrons are eager to see him capitulate or curious to see whether he can gouge you or not.

"Deal." You pull nine silver from your pocket. He takes the coin from the top of the bar with no smirk. It seems you got a fair deal.

He turns to a pot sitting over a fire and fills a wooden bowl with stew. He passes it across the bar to you. "Drink will be extra."

A gnome on a stool to your left laughs. "Drink is always extra."

The other nearby patrons laugh with him.

You find yourself laughing with the rest. "No drink tonight. I'm weary from the road."

The barkeep nods and hands you an iron key. "Second floor, third door on the right."

You dip your head graciously and step away from the bar, carrying your bowl of stew with you. Carefully, you carry it past other patrons and tables of dice and cards. Out of the tavern and up the stairs to your room, you insert the key into the door.

As the wood swings open, a little room is revealed. Nothing special. A lamp glistens on a table with two little chairs beside the window. A clean-looking bed rests on the other side beside a little table with a mirror. A clean bowl of water and some cloth rests on top. Yes, this is most certainly a nice inn along a well-traveled road.

You step inside and close the door behind you. You sigh as you settle in one of the chairs. Your hand shakes a little as you pull the soup spoon to your mouth and you get your first taste of freshly-cooked meat in weeks. It is delightfully salty and warm. You long to savor the taste in your mouth longer before it slides down your throat, but then it warms your belly and you are too content to care anymore.

When your dinner is complete, you carefully rest your bowl outside your room and ensure the door is locked when you shut it for the night. You peel your dirty clothes off and wash yourself with the basin of water beside the bed. It feels delightful to pull cleaner clothes on a washed body.

Glancing out the window, night has fallen. You can no longer see the tall mountains or forest surrounding this little valley and village.

Pulling back the sheets, you settle onto a thin yet comfortable mattress. No sticks. No cold, rocky ground. You fall asleep almost instantly.

During my chemotherapy treatment, the creative part of my brain shut down. For a writer who is always thinking up new characters and new plot ideas, this was the most disorienting sensation. It was worse than the very worst writer's block. It was like a voice in my head had been silenced. A water spout turned to only the barest drip. I lacked the words to explain what I was feeling, so instead things just "went missing."

During my treatment, I barely looked at my writing documents, let alone tried to type anything new down. I didn't even feel like reading other people's books, and looking back that was…super weird. Instead the days were full of discomfort and pain. We would watch movies and TV shows, mostly to distract ourselves and pass the time without having to move from the couch. My boss even commented that my designs for work were not as detailed or appealing as before. No joke.

As my brain came back online a few weeks after the end of my chemotherapy treatment, I noticed that gradual drip of my creative spout turn to a deluge. It was at that moment that I realized what had been missing for months, because before, I hadn't been able to put a name to it. Creativity had been muted and muddled by disease.

One of the best moments was having my first book idea in months. It was a REALLY good one. It shaped an amazing change in the trajectory of the entire series. It made a few plot holes finally work. I woke up early (something I had consistently struggled to do) and wrote and wrote and wrote. I love what I do for my nine to five, but it does not compare to getting to sit down and creatively pen my tales.

Writing stories does not exhaust me. Yes, having writer's block is a thing, but when one story isn't coming, I just write a different one until I can come back with fresh eyes. I kid you not, I have four major series ideas running and several more screenplays. I feel like Hamilton. How do you write like tomorrow won't arrive? Because there are so many stories in my head just waiting to be unleashed.

We all have things we are skilled in. Maybe it's public speaking or art or mathematics or sports or discipline. Having the active opportunities to use our proficiencies can lead to extremely better outcomes. Not only might we succeed better or faster, but we probably will enjoy the journey more immensely. When things start to come easier, where it doesn't feel like we are fighting up the mountain or through the dark forest, a sense of flow can be reached. Pursuing a goal can feel less like a fight and more like an adventure.

So many of us have never felt this sense of flow, because we are pulled away from what we are best at or what we love to do due to expectation. It is our responsibility in this fight for the fairytale to give ourselves more opportunities to do more of what we are good at. Not only does this feel good on the inside, but it also can help us see success faster.

For a fiction reference, if you have watched the anime *Black Clover*, would Asta have any success if he kept trying to perform magic like Yuno? Absolutely not. His power was that he was devoid of magic. His power was his willingness to train and hone his body. His power was never giving up.

Nesta in *A Court of Silver Flames* kept inviting the priestesses to train with her, even when they kept failing to show up. She kept trying to walk the 10,000 stairs even when her body failed on 100. While stubbornness could be a deficiency, we can see how she made it a proficiency.

The things we are good at need to be embraced. Only when they are embraced can they show us the path forward—remind us of the possibility.

So if you have been languishing in this place of "I'm not good at anything"—this is your chance to flip the switch.

We will discuss this topic more when it's time to decide what fairytale you are fighting for, but just think about it for a second now. You might have circled a few already. What do you love doing? Can you be doing more of that? Does that activity require a sort of skill? Get your mind thinking, and we will return to it shortly.

SIDE QUEST:

For the introverts among us, this might be the most difficult step yet. Because we so often are blinded by our own self-deprecation or self-doubt or self-criticism, we often cannot see where our strengths truly lie. Luckily, the other people close to us can see through this veil.

You are going to choose three to ten people. I know this may sound like a lot, especially if you are fairly introverted and keep your circle small. If that's the case, lean toward three. If you are up to the challenge, lean toward ten. The number here matters because we are going to want to correlate what MANY people say, versus one or two who may give you a skewed impression.

You will choose only people who are extremely close to you, who you trust completely. Think of the people that encourage you, support you, and inspire you. Think of the people that you feel you can be your whole self around. These are the people to ask.

You are going to ask them a few questions:

1. What do they love about you?
2. Why do they enjoy spending time with you?
3. What skills do you have that inspire or awe them?

You can ask each person all three or sprinkle the questions out among them. If you can physically see or visit them, ask these questions in person. If you feel up to a phone call, do it. If not, or if this entire exercise is downright nerve-wracking, a text or an email works just fine.

See what they say.

Jot it down on the next page in your notebook.

There is no judgment. Just jot it down.

Hopefully, these words will warm your heart.

It is often surprising to hear the little things about ourselves that we often overlook be so honored by our loved ones.

The idea is that we, too, should tell our loved ones these things more often. We shouldn't wait to say them at a funeral when they can no longer hear. No, we need to tell people why we love them, why we enjoy them, why we are amazed and inspired by them. Now.

We go so long never hearing it. It is a lack in this hard and cruel world, but we can fill it.

So ask for their words. Don't be ashamed. Don't hesitate.

If they respond, thank them for being open and honest with you. Offer to tell them your answers for them if they would like. If they say yes, send your thoughtful reply. Just this tiny effort could create a world of good.

SESSION RECAP:

Now that you have the words from your friends and family before you, let's start to develop a new skill together. Let's evaluate the list of things people have said about you. Which ones do you agree with? Which ones don't you see? You can highlight the comments in two different colors—those you agree with and those you don't—if that helps you visually.

After you have done that, again sit back and consider the colors. Is there more you agree with? Or do your friends and family see you in a completely different light?

Take a little time to journal about the ideas, feelings, and comments that pop up during this exercise. For now, we just use this as a tool to get closer to ourselves, but eventually this will help you decide on your first fairytale.

This is the skill of discernment. Which skills do you believe will help you achieve your fairytale?

Will you keep pursuing the things your friends and family say you are good at? Or do you want to be known for something else, something different?

Are you going to fight to develop skills that are challenging to you because they excite you? Or are you going to find a different path with a skill you are already proficient in?

All options are valid, so long as you pursue them with an open heart and a conscious mind.

In the comfort of the inn, a long night's rest comes to you. It is welcome and warm. Though you have been having frightening and haunting dreams, none of them come for you. Perhaps they are scared off by the pleasant tavern din downstairs, or maybe they cannot breach the wooden walls of the inn, but you are grateful either way.

When you awake, you sigh with pleasure. This is a nice bed in a nice tavern. You got it for nine silver! Yes, this kind of maneuvering in the town is definitely more up your alley. You have always been a bit more of a talker. You can read people well. You know how to be tough but fair.

It may not seem like the best skill in the world, but it has certainly served you tonight and others in the past. No doubt it will serve you again in the future.

With a smile on your face, you stretch and give yourself another hour.

The Shiny & The Useful

"Not all treasure is silver and gold, mate."

FROM JACK SPARROW IN WALT DISNEY
PICTURES PIRATES OF THE CARIBBEAN:
THE CURSE OF THE BLACK PEARL

You rise as the light grows in your room from the window. You sit up
and stretch. The room is warm with the glowing morning light, and
you relish the warmth of the sheets and blankets around you. You give
yourself a few minutes to just sit. Your feet still ache, but your back
feels glorious! No cold bones!

You rise and set your feet on the floorboards. You cross the room
to the window and stare out at the surrounding town, fields, and
mountains beyond. The day is dawning, golden. Below, you can see
the villagers already moving about their tasks. Fruit and vegetable
stands are open in the wide village square. The blacksmith is already
hammering at their anvil.

You watch it all. It's like a little anthill. You are watching the ants
work.

Then, suddenly, that pit sinks back down into the middle of your stomach. Where are you? What are you going to do now? The shadow is clinging to you again.

You swallow down the fear that is coming up. Yes, this is a new town. You don't even know the name, but it is calm and safe. You will spend a few days, learn what you can, and then set off again. This is a step in the adventure. You have to take each step to get to the next. That is what it means to journey.

Your fear successfully chastised, you dress and gather a light smattering of your belongings, leaving the larger pack behind for now and locking your door behind you as you exit.

You step down into the tavern below. It is fairly quiet. The revelers of the night before are either gone or still asleep upstairs. A few laborers appear to be finishing up a hot plate. A grizzly old man already grips a tankard.

The barkeep sees you enter the room and steps away. You sit down at the bar, and he returns with a fresh plate of sausages and eggs.

"Breakfast as promised," he says.

You nod in thanks and once again devour the meal that is set before you until it's hot in your belly.

Then, you gather up your belongings and head out to join the rest of the ants that you watched from above.

It takes you less than thirty minutes to traverse the main thoroughfare through the village from north to south and back again. You peer into the shop windows and people-watch while eating a loaf of bread from the baker. The village feels much like your own, the one you left behind. Just families going about their daily lives.

However, this town is clearly a wayside along the great road. Every manner of folk and creature can be seen wandering through or just passing by. You've seen elves and dwarves. You've seen humans in garments you have never even imagined before. These are people from every walk of life. From all over the world. Your friends had said you would see that if you followed the great road. It is well-traveled and lively, yet risky for the solo traveler. That was why you had avoided it. But now, in the town, you have the pleasure of embracing it.

You find your eyes pulled back to the largest shop in town. A general store, but with two stories and shiny baubles glinting in the front windows. It wouldn't hurt to go look. You could use to refill on rations.

As you enter the door, a light bell jingles above. The shopkeep looks up from where he is polishing his front counter.

"Ah, welcome! Come in! Come in!" He gathers his robes and puffs up his chest. "Welcome to my emporium!"

You nod your head again in greeting, hating being the center of attention, but there are no other customers in the store to distract him.

"Looking for anything in particular?" he continues. "I have everything the traveler might need from traveling clothes, better boots, food rations, even a weapon or two if you are looking for something of a magical sort."

"Magical?" you question. The word piques your interest.

"Yes! Yes! If it's a magical item you are looking for, you have come to the right place!" He carefully ducks down below the counter and rummages. He pulls up a box and several small vials. Then he turns and grabs a sword from the wall behind him. "Come see! Come see!"

You walk closer to inspect his wares.

"This," he begins, lifting up the small box. "This contains several small candles that burn without being consumed! Very nice, very handy. You will never have to worry about purchasing candles again."

"That seems arcane in nature," you note shrewdly. "I am no practitioner."

"Ah, ah, I see. Well, I could teach you the word that lights them. For an extra fee, of course."

"Perhaps." You nod. It would be nice to have a few of those around, even if the enchantment did not last forever. You could at least have a little light to read by on those nights in the woods when you couldn't light a proper fire. Maybe you could even trade him for your flint and steel—the useless thing.

In your consideration, the shopkeeper has already moved on to bigger and better things. "And these vials each contain a serum of strength. Drink this, and you will have the strength of ten men!"

"How long does that last?"

The man nods, readjusting his robes again. "Ten minutes."

"Ah."

"Very, very helpful, you know, when you are in a sticky situation. Or maybe need to move something very heavy. The masons buy them sometimes to help move foundation stones."

"No, no thank you."

The sword has caught your eye. It glints in the sunlight, crafted of reflecting metals of silver and gold. The shopkeeper notices your gaze.

"This," he says. "This is the finest weapon you will find on this side of mountains." He draws the blade from the scabbard and presents it to you with regal holiness. "It will guide you to your strongest path. You will know the road ahead like you lived there all your life."

You try not to show it, but this has shocked you. This is the best thing you have ever heard. After the daunting journey so far and being lost in the woods, you don't know what the path forward looks like. Here is an item that can tell you! How fortuitous! A weapon like that just sitting and waiting for you here in this shop. It's like the fates knew you needed it.

You grasp the weapon. You don't really know swords, but it feels well balanced, well made to you. You step back and swing it tentatively back and forth.

"Ah," a voice speaks in your mind. "Now here is a great and virtuous adventurer."

Your shock must now be registering on your face, because the shopkeeper chuckles. "Yes, it quite literally tells you your strongest path. What is it telling you?"

"You are destined for great things. A great many things," the sword continues. "Both here and far across the sea."

"I'm destined to travel across the sea?" you question out loud.

"Yes," the sword answers. "You will win many a great battle, both on and off the sea, young warrior."

Winning great battles?

"The sea is a wonderful, massive thing," the man physically before you includes. "Oh, if you are headed to the sea, I also have this tonic. This will help ease any seasickness you may experience."

"How much?" you ask of the sword.

"Seven hundred and fifty gold."

Geez. That is about as much as you've got. "I will give you five hundred."

The shopkeeper frowns. "I told you this is the finest sword this side of the mountains."

Okay, he's ready to play.

You smile. "Good thing I am headed to the other side of the mountains."

The man chuckles lightly, remaining good-natured. "Seven hundred gold. This weapon will guide you on your strongest path, both in life and through the mountains you still face to get to the other side."

The voice of the sword grows louder, like it is cheering for you. "And you will taste the blood of your enemies!"

Ah, the shiny object syndrome. We've all been there. From glossy social media marketing to eloquent salespeople, we all are prone to pursue the next big, bright, beautiful thing. And the next. And the next. Month to month it seems we cannot focus. If we get the thing we have been craving and pining after, on we move to the next.

Shiny object syndrome is intensely dangerous on our journey to fight for our fairytale because it's a magic sword telling us to set down something we want most for something else we want sooner. Do you want to taste the blood of your enemies? Or do you just want to move forward on an adventure? I would think most of us aren't lusting for blood. Thanks, talking sword!

Why spend years in school getting a degree when you can put your trust in an unvetted, faster online course from a popular YouTuber, right?

Why work through a difficult patch in your relationship when you can ditch it for a new, fresh one on a dating site?

Fighting for the fairytale requires patience, diligence, and consistent effort. Often, it is at first going to be front-loaded, tons of work without seeing a payoff. Sorry, no instant gratification, but over time, with focus, the fairytale will be molded and shaped.

During my time working in real estate, I saw this very often. Some of the best and brightest newly-licensed realtors pass through the doors of brokerages. At our office, we coached, planned, and strategized. It truly worked with time and effort. The results flowed back to us. Then, some wanted results faster, easier, with less effort. They'd see an ad online or attend a seminar and suddenly believe a $1,000+ course was the thing that was going to change the trajectory of their business forever. While they took the course, what fell to the wayside? The strategies and the daily to-dos that were steadily and consistently building their business from the ground up. A year or two later, where did we stand? Alas, $1,000 poorer and right where we stopped a year prior.

Personally, for a long time, my shiny object syndrome was about buying the next new things that would supposedly help me get fit or get the body I desired. It was the right gym membership, the right tool, the right workout clothes, the right trainer—but in the end, all that mattered was me showing up in the gym. Consistency was key, and far, far cheaper. When that clicked, my body actually did start to change.

Harry Potter did not immediately grasp the spell Expecto Patronum, despite being the chosen one. It took consistent practice, even when it sucked the life out of him. Even when it left him panting and exhausted on the floor waiting for Lupin to pass him a bit of chocolate. In the end, it took belief in his own ability, knowledge that he was capable of anything he set his mind to, in order to cast the spell and save himself in the woods that night. No shiny object. No magic fix. Just hard work and effort.

As you learn to fight for your fairytale, you will learn to fight the shiny object syndrome. The more in tune you are with yourself and your biggest goals, the easier it will be to reject the objects that aren't for you. You will also come to learn which shiny objects are actually valuable to you and worth your resources. When you have a clear head and clear focus, you can be the gold miner sifting through the sand to find *your gold*, not the gems someone else told you that you should value.

SIDE QUEST:

In all likelihood, some of your shiny objects might still exist inside your home. It's the book you never read and likely never will because it was all about becoming a dog trainer—when you wanted to do that—and now you would rather just spend time with your own little pooch than work to train other people's. It is the protein powder you don't really like the taste of and is already expired in the back of your cabinet that was going to help you grow those massive muscles. It's the subscription to the online education portal that you pay for month after month saying you are going to learn it, but now you don't really care to.

Like the clutter in your house back in Level Two that we took a little time to clear up, are these old shiny objects cluttering up your mind? Do they remind you day in and day out about the dreams you once had? Or the dreams you once thought you *should have*? Are they putting a pressure on you to do something that might distract you from beginning to build your true fairytale?

If you answered yes to any of these, now is the time to set down this book and gather them up. Yes, starting with that expired protein powder! Get rid of it! The process of getting rid of these physical items also serves as a way to provide you with a mental declutter and help you organize your thoughts toward the future.

If some of these things are something you might want to come back to, something that might become a part of your fairytale, you can keep them. However, instead of them lying around in places of prominence where they can distract you, these old shiny objects are going in a box, out of sight, out of mind, until you are ready for them! When that time comes, we will pull them back out.

Maybe you will want to be a dog trainer after all!

SESSION RECAP:

Alright, we are heading back with our favorite characters. Leona, are you with me? Of course, you are.

What are some of the shiny objects your favorite characters fell to pursue? Was it a throne? A partner? A grand idea?

What made those shiny objects not last? How did your favorite characters come to realize they were made of plastic and not gold?

What made your characters grow and persist, and ultimately, leave them behind?

Those questions are interesting to think about because though the characters we look up to may have magic qualities or even be a "chosen one," more often than not they are just like us, they have real flaws and failings that tend to mess life up.

So, how do our favorite characters cope when faced with a challenge? How do they reach their next goal?

If you are a fantasy reader like me, it was probably meticulous practice, honing their body out in the woods, soaking up knowledge in a library. Any money needed there? No, probably not most of the time.

Before the tragedy of vampires struck her village, Leona spent her days learning from her uncle, a wise elder warrior in their clan. She ran and trained her body. She competed against her friends and fellow warriors. She kept up with her studies, allowed her smart elder brother and disciplined father to teach her languages and maths and histories.

What does it boil down to? Consistency. Consistently building along a path. *A pursuit of becoming.* I think we can all learn from that.

Your silence must have been long because the shopkeeper speaks again. "Seven hundred gold and I will throw in the tonic against seasickness."

You gingerly set the talking sword back down on the counter. Somehow, tasting the blood of your enemies was not specifically on your to-do list or even among your lifelong goals. That was a part of adventuring that you were always a little skittish of. No, the talking sword is definitely not the voice you want beside you on the wide, empty road.

"Actually, I'll consider those candles instead."

The shopkeeper shakes his head. "Really? Oh, well you can have those for twenty-five gold."

"Twenty-five?"

"Yes, plus another five to learn the magic word that makes them light."

"No way. Twenty gold total. For the lot."

You meet the shopkeeper's stare. You watch him consider his odds behind his eyes. "Aye, right enough."

You hand him the money, and he hands you the box and the magic word. You step out of the emporium into the sunlight and find yourself sweating.

You really considered buying that dumb magic sword! A talking sword that wanted you to kill! How narrowly you avoided buying the blasted thing! Insane to think a person (or a talking sword) could weasel their way in and convince you that you needed something you didn't. It all sounded so shiny and pretty.

You tuck your candles away into your pack and realize you failed to purchase any rations, something you actually needed! No way are you going back into that emporium. That shopkeep would never give you another deal.

Instead, you set back out around town, hoping you will find another place that can provide you for the road ahead.

Stocking Up For When You Need It Most

"Come, potion, lend me vigor!"

FROM VICTOR SALTZPYRE IN FAT SHARK'S
WARHAMMER VERMINTIDE II

An hour or so later, you find yourself paused before the apothecary. You slow down and watch a small beetle crawl its way up a vine that decorates the outside of the shop. Like a maze it winds up the main branch of the vine, occasionally getting lost in the shorter branches and leaves that depart to the sides. It finally settles for a leaf a little bit above your eyeline. It nearly glows in the bright sunshine. You shift closer to watch and it buzzes at you, but sensing you don't mean it any harm, it settles and begins munching on the corner of the leaf. You smile at the little squiggles it leaves on the edge.

Around you is a covered porch to the right of a small display window filled with crystals and candles. Above hang hundreds of different dried herbs and plants, swinging softly in the light breeze, soaking in the sunshine. There is an aroma in the air, something sweet yet earthy.

You step inside the store to find it filled with a surprising number of both clientele and attendants. You relish in the ability to sink into the background and explore the full shelves and the wares without attention.

There is an assortment of odd knick-knacks and balms and salves. There are carefully labeled pastes and vials of liquid. You explore the crystals in the shop window.

All the while, the shop is bustling with activity. A young woman sets carefully to the task of haggling with a gnome, bartering for some strange sticks of incense. An elderly man works in the back, just in view in another room, grinding with a mortar and pestle. A small child with horns holds their wrist with tears in their eyes before a healer woman, who leans over and whispers a few words. The tears fade and the child wiggles their fingers, broken wrist mended. The healer touches the child's face and hurries them along outside, dropping a small candy made of honey in their hand.

The feel of this place is quiet and calming, almost like a sanctuary.

You grab a lemon salve for the cracked skin on your feet and two potions of healing, making your way toward the front to wait your turn to make your purchases.

You barely get a few steps when the door opens again. A tall elf enters with long, dark hair with braided pieces framing his face. He's broad and strong. The leathers he wears are so dark they are almost black. His skin is pale, near sickly. The sunshine in the room almost seems to dissipate a little. The others in the apothecary don't seem to notice it, but you have certainly grown attuned to changes in light the past few weeks.

You watch the elf stride across the room, assured, barely using the staff he holds in one hand as a walking stick. You notice that he is starkly missing his left arm. He doesn't even hide it with his cloak flipped back over his shoulders.

When he reaches the counter, the healer meets his gaze and studies him. She frowns heavily as he speaks quietly and recites a list of ingredients and herbs he needs.

The woman refuses at first. He argues, and then the rest of the room becomes aware of the darkness drawn to this man. The gnome glances worriedly to the side. The elderly man has stopped grinding to peek out to the front of the shop.

The elf slaps a bag of gold on the table and gestures pointedly.

Slowly, the woman nods and disappears into another room at the back of the shop, clearly some sort of storage space.

This is the point where the elf spins slowly and nearly makes eye contact with you. You drop your gaze down, pretending to be interested in another shelf of wares while you wait to be attended to.

He turns further and seems to inspect the rest of the store. Carefully, the other workers continue on their tasks, but they keep him in their peripheral vision, too.

The healer returns with a small satchel. You can hear the contents shift as she sets it on the counter and takes the bag of gold. The elf nods and departs.

The shop holds its breath for several moments after his presence disappears.

Then, the woman waves you over and considers your purchases. "Well, that's refreshing."

"What is?" you ask.

"Just some normal, perfectly good items. 115 gold." You fish in your bag for the sum. You have no desire to haggle with her, especially not when she clearly has to deal with some less-than-favorable clientele. The woman continues to study you. "Prone to cracked skin or—"

"Oh, my feet," you begin. "I've been on the road a while."

"Well," the woman continues as she takes your gold, "mixing that salve with some extra lard will help seal up anything already cracked. When your feet aren't cracked, just use a little bit to moisturize the skin, especially if you are going to be walking more."

"Yes, I have a feeling more walking is in my future."

The healer smiles to herself. "Always for you adventuring types."

To rip off the British phrase of resilience and a popular meme, "Keep calm and carry a healing potion."

Having a health potion would be pretty convenient, right? You are telling me that when I sprained my ankle, I could drink a vial of liquid and immediately erase the pain and even the injury itself? What if it worked on other things besides injuries? What if you could clear up a cold or even fight off cancer?

I'm sure I would be willing to spend more than a pretty penny to have magic like that available to me, especially since we never hear about any side effects.

The crazy thing about chemotherapy is that in some ways the treatment is even more painful and invasive than the disease is. When I had cancer in my body, it was just a lump that sometimes bothered me when I lay on it. Sure, it was probably causing a lot of other long-term harm, and had I left it to grow it certainly would have created bigger problems. However, when I found my Stage II breast cancer, it really was not affecting my daily life very much at all.

However, the instant I started my chemo, the treatment decided to beat me up. Those side effects I mentioned, yeah, I got a bunch of them. To start, I had an allergic reaction to one of my chemo drugs within a few minutes on my first treatment. It made it hard to breathe and my throat and skin itchy. My family tends to not be button pushers, so my mom had to literally tell me to push the emergency button to call the nurse. It was so outside of my nature to call attention to myself, I felt embarrassed when the nurses came running. I didn't even think that my life might be in danger. When their eyes widened, though, and someone called for an oxygen tank, I knew that this was going to be a new situation for me.

For the rest of my months of treatment, I would be sleepy and hopped up on Benadryl to contradict the effects of that side effect. The chemo drug combination was just too perfect for my type of cancer for the doctors NOT to put something I was allergic to into my body. Scary, right?

Next, I lost my hair. They had said it would start to fall out at the three week mark if I didn't try cold capping—a process where you put a dry ice frozen skull cap on your head for the entirety of your treatment. At first, I considered the process. We even bought the expensive system. However, since my treatment started the day after Labor Day, no dry ice facilities were open. I said 'screw it' because I felt like we were more worried about looking for dry ice than taking care of my health. So, I accepted the fact that my hair would fall out. Like clockwork, my beautiful, long, waist-length curly locks started to pull out in the shower. Piece by piece we pulled out my hair, until it was getting so thin, knotty, and sparse that I said "enough." We shaved it off the next day.

Though nausea was not on my main list of symptoms, diarrhea definitely was. That unfortunate side effect led to loss of appetite and dehydration. I ended up having to go in for fluids once or twice a week after each infusion. Again, I worried I was a burden showing up at the cancer center so often to have saline pushed into my system through the port. However, as treatment continued, and I passed out a few times, ended up in the emergency room with a potential stroke, and constantly dealt with a lack of energy, I realized this was the monster of my symptoms. By the last treatment, I found myself sitting silently in the chair for fluids realizing how grateful I was for the lovely nurses who treated me day in and day out. They made me feel welcome and comfortable, and that's a blessing in and of itself.

Despite all the side effects that chemotherapy inflicted on my body, these drugs were still a magic potion in my book. When chemotherapy was complete, my cancer was 100% gone—only scar tissue left behind. That is pretty incredible.

What if we had healing potions that were 100% side effect free? Even though the magic potions don't exist outside of our video games and RPG campaigns, isn't there a way for them to exist in a different capacity? What would those look like in our life? Leaving aside prescribed pharmaceuticals, drugs, and alcohol, what are the positive things that can give us a boost and help us feel better or have an edge?

As we prepare to set out on the journey of Part Two, having your health potions purchased or prepared is going to be integral in your enjoyment of the adventure.

So, what do you actually need? For all humans, we need our physiological needs to be met—food, water, shelter, sleep. Then, we can address our mental and emotional ones. When we are in our dark night of the soul, these small needs being met can actually become comfort to lift us out of the darkness just enough that we are able to get back on our feet again. So, start with the basics. Maybe make a checklist.

Have I eaten a healthy meal with fruits and vegetables today?

Have I drunk a glass (or eight) of water?

Do I need a nap? Have I prioritized sleep as much as I can?

Once these basics are fulfilled, we can turn to our health potions.

The health potions are going to be a lot more fun. Unlike having our physical needs met, the health potions will be the things that address our mental and emotional needs, help us feel better, or bring us enjoyment. The idea is, with all the work you are doing, you need to have some fun, too.

So, how can you take a health potion in your real life when you need it?

One of my greatest comforts is having a clean and organized house. I mentioned its proportional nature to my mental state earlier, and it's true! The happier I am, the tidier I am. So getting into a system for maintaining organization and cleanliness in my home has helped me maintain a higher level of happiness day to day in my fight for the fairytale.

I have drafted a few sample lists, that might be very specific to me, just so you can start catching a glimpse at what your health potions may look like. The important thing is that you have something special set aside just for when you need a boost in fighting for your fairytale. So try to pick things that you would not normally eat, use, or buy. This should be a treat, but it doesn't have to be. Your health potions could also be a comfort item that you turn to frequently.

Your health potions can be simple pleasures. They don't need to cost a thing. What your list contains will be completely unique to you! We will get to building your health potions in the journaling portion of this chapter. Think of it as the fantasy, fighting for your fairytale version of self-care!

Items I might purchase and keep in the house:

- A special non-alcoholic beverage

- A favorite snack

- A scented candle

- A lotion or bath bomb

- A new book

- Ingredients to bake my favorite dessert or cook my favorite meal

- Leave my yoga mat out and ready to grab

Activities I might schedule or engage in:

- A visit to the library

- An in-house movie night or trip to the theater

- A new class at a yoga studio or an art studio

- A designated time for an uninterrupted hot bath

- A game night with friends or family

- An in-person or Zoom dinner (make it a mukbang even) with a friend

SESSION RECAP:

We are switching up the order again because it might be of more use to you to make a list and then be able to decide what special items you are collecting to be your health potions.

Here are the questions to reflect on:

1. What are the things and activities that provide you with the most comfort?
2. What makes you feel the best when you are down?
3. Is there a way that you can have them on hand and make them easy to access when you are in your difficult or dark moments?

Don't feel silly or selfish about these little things. Little comforts in a big and terrifying world are extremely necessary.

Something that sounds particularly good at the moment is making my own special coffee and laughing at my own failed attempts at latte art. So, go on, once you have reflected on the questions above, make your own two lists of potential health potions—"items to keep in the home" and "activities to plan to engage in."

SIDE QUEST:

Now onto the action! This one should be easy! Go and purchase or gather one or two of your health potions. Once you have done that, give them a special and designated place in your home. If it's food, maybe you clean off a little section of shelf or set it in a beautiful container on the door of your fridge. If it's art supplies, maybe a section of your desk gets to be your easily accessible display.

No matter what your health potions are, try to keep them in a place of prominence. The more you see them, the more you will think about the enjoyment they bring you. They can be something to look forward to using or something to have in case of emergencies. No matter what, with your preparation, they will be there waiting to help you fight for your fairytale!

The young woman behind the counter speaks next as her gnomish customer leaves the apothecary. "That's the second person wandering in here looking for ingredients to deter vampires," she mutters quietly to the healer beside her. You are not sure if she means to include you, but you insert yourself in the conversation anyway.

"Deter vampires?"

"You think we've got a problem?" the healer asks her coworker.

"Haven't heard of any threat of vampires in the village. Or nearby."

The healer leans back, crossing her arms with one hip on the counter. "This one seemed like a part of the problem. Last one, I had hoped was a solution."

The young woman shrugs and turns to you. "If you are planning to head out on the road again anytime soon, I would make some extra preparations."

"Preparations?"

"Traveling with a group?"

"No, I've been on my own," you answer.

"I would consider finding yourself a traveling party. Even a temporary one. Someone to guard your back, especially at night. If there are vampires about, they're no joke."

You had never considered it: traveling with a group of strangers. It would be convenient and perhaps helpful—surely another person would have the necessary skills to light a fire for you. You guess, though, that would mean having to figure out where you are headed and why.

"Thanks, I'll keep it in mind."

The young woman nods and shifts back to her work. "There's a fight tonight at the tavern. Sure if you make yourself known you will come across someone looking for company on the road."

You nod your head, pocket your goods, and make your way out of the apothecary.

Q&A = Quests & Advice

"Every time I'm near you, I say more
in five minutes than I've said in
weeks. And I always regret it."

FROM GERALT OF RIVIA IN NETFLIX'S
THE WITCHER TV SERIES

That night when you return to the tavern with the setting of the sun, you open the door to find it packed, even more so than the night before. There is a raucous shouting from the far end of the room. A crowd stands in a circle, looking down into a pit you had not realized was there before. As you get closer, you see that where the pit now sinks down, the night before there had been tables. The floorboards and supports were pulled away tonight to reveal the fighting pit below. A clever use of space; you have never seen such a setup.

Inside the ring, a half orc fights a human with roiled muscles. Both are fighting with fists. The human is quite strong and rather lumbering. He lands a solid punch to the orc's temple that would have knocked you out cold for hours. The orc gathers herself and dashes quickly. Her speed alone makes up for what she might lack in size compared to the human. She lands a solid kick to the side of the human's knee. The crowd erupts in "oohs," gritted teeth, smiles, and laughter.

You watch them go until the orc rattles her final punch and the human collapses to the dirt.

All around you the tavern-goers cheer or groan and haul the orc out of the pit. They push her to the bar, where the barkeep pours her a drink on the house. She drains it and the crowd erupts again, invigorated. There is a heavy passing of coin—wagers and bets made and lost.

The room settles again as patrons wrap themselves around tables and card games. You think that perhaps the fighting is over for the night, but clearly that was just one round of many. A bookie-type peddler walks table to table, showing off the list of competitors for the evening and collecting more coin as people test the odds.

Another pair enters the ring, both thin and gangly. You watch the tavern-goers shift back to the circle as the next fighters bounce and swing, preparing for their go.

You decide instead that this is your chance to head over to the bar and claim your meal.

Lacking other patrons at the moment, the barkeep quickly turns to you. "Dinner?" You nod yes and he departs for the back room and returns with a chicken leg and roasted potatoes. "You drinking tonight?" he asks as he sets the plate before you.

"Actually, yes."

The barkeep dips his head and grabs a tankard, filling it to the brim with ale. "Specialty of the house."

You set to eating silently as the barkeep grabs a cloth and polishes the countertop.

Midway through your meal, you finally decide to ask him, "The woman at the apothecary was saying there's been an uptick of people in the village looking for ingredients to deter vampires. Have you heard anything about it?"

The barkeep pauses in his cleaning. "Aye, there was a vampire hunter passing through a few days ago. She said she was on the tail of some sort of mob of 'em."

"A mob? That's concerning."

"Aye, but her and her companions assured us they wouldn't be coming into town. They had already passed us, through the mountains to our west."

"She makes a living? Just hunting vampires?"

"She didn't stick around and I didn't ask."

A dwarf a few stools down meets your eyes. "Not sure if you can make your way just hunting vampires, but she had the look of a monster hunter about her. Plenty of that to go around."

The barkeep nods. "Sure is. Got a sign board full of 'em. Just over there." He tilts his head toward a board on the back wall filled with flyers and papers. "Anything you are looking for in terms of work, you will find it there—from farmhands and sheep herding to personal guards and monster hunting." He fills a few more tankards and pushes them down the bar to some other patrons who have gathered there before he returns to stand before you. "My advice, snag something that will keep you moving in the direction you're headed. Make some coin and continue on your way."

"Thanks."

"You seem new to it. To traveling."

"It is something new."

"Well, keep it simple. No need to bite off more than you can chew."

Sometimes the very best ideas come unexpectedly and out of the blue. If you enter a tavern in a video game, you are guaranteed to hit the small talk of the patrons, but if you head to the bar and talk to the tavern keeper, there is always a new side quest waiting for you to accept. While side quests don't always help you reach your main goals, they sure have a way of finding you magical items, coin, or at least experience points that can help you along the way when you course correct and get back to your original goal again.

Entering the tavern in a video game or RPG campaign is a lot like putting yourself in a new locale in your real life. Whether you go off to school, join a new club, attend a new exercise class, go to that networking event, or agree to the blind date, suddenly there are new faces, new backstories, new opportunities, and new adventures surrounding you. These are wonderful opportunities to open yourself to new advice and new quests. You never know where inspiration is going to hit from.

When you put yourself a little out of your comfort zone, it can do wonders for setting a new adventure under your feet. That's exactly what we are looking for here! Think of it as a real life call to adventure. This isn't necessarily as big as Katniss volunteering for her sister in *The Hunger Games* or the Hightowers stealing the crown from Rhaenyra in *House of Dragon*. It can literally be something as small as trying that new TV show that your new acquaintances recommend.

When my Dungeon Master first introduced me to RPG, she suggested a one-shot so we could all dip our toes in. All three players at the table had never played the game before, but we had varying levels of familiarity with the concept. In the beginning, I was terrified of role-play. I remember the first few minutes of the game when she was playing a character we met in a tavern, introducing us to the mission, and she asked me a question about myself in character. It was so hard to answer! I remember how my stomach turned. I was *so* out of my comfort zone. When we finished the one-shot, we all had enjoyed ourselves enough to say yes to an official campaign, but our one rule, more combat and less role-play.

Well, we didn't stop trying, and now look at me. Several years later with Level Fourteen characters, and we are still playing that campaign. You would be proud of me. I'm role-playing and pursuing an NPC romance even. All of it! For goodness sake, now I am writing a book on the topic, forcing you readers into a small bit of role-play. It is amazing how putting ourselves in new situations and opening ourselves up to understanding the things that other people enjoy expands our minds and hearts to things that we ourselves might enjoy, too.

SIDE QUEST:

In the next week, put yourself in one new situation.

If you love books but have had trouble reading when you keep getting pulled back to your Netflix queue, find a book club to join at the local library. If you always knit or crochet by yourself, join a group and try a new or more challenging design. I have heard there are a lot of cool opportunities online, so you don't even have to leave your house! If you always hang out with a certain group of friends, look through your contact list and find an old schoolmate who you haven't connected with in ages to get a coffee with. If you are young, talk to an older coworker or one of your parents' friends about their experiences when they were your age. If you are older, call a grandchild, niece, or nephew and genuinely listen to them talk about their school, job, friends, or things they enjoy.

The options are endless.

The idea is that when you put yourself with someone new or in a new place, that you both mentally and physically will not be able to easily do things as you have always done them. You will be forced to consider something you never have before.

So when you put yourself in that new situation, one that is safe but slightly out of your comfort zone, make a pledge that you will move into this situation with an open mind and an open heart. Pledge that you are ready to absorb what this event has to teach. Be attentive. Be observant. Try to talk to people and learn their stories. I am excited to see what comes up for you.

SESSION RECAP:

Alrighty, extroverts, it is time to chill out and come back to rest. Introverts, welcome back to your safe space by yourself. Now is our time to reflect on the new experience you had. Take five to ten minutes to write a paragraph or two about all the details of the experience, or maybe some bullet points.

Here are some prompts to help you get to thinking and writing.

- What new situation did you encounter?

- What was the location like? Sights? Sounds? Smells?

- Did you meet any new people? What were they like?

- Did anyone tell you a unique or interesting story?

- Was there anything that stood out to you or that you felt particularly connected to?

- How do you feel now that you are home or out of that situation?

- Would you want to experience it again?

  ▷ If yes, how will you craft your plan to do it again? Will you schedule it? Sign up for another class? Call another friend, etc.?

  ▷ If no, why was that experience not fun for you? What would make it better? What could you explore instead?

This is also a great opportunity to start creating a list of new experiences or past experiences that you have a passion for and would want to explore in the future. What are those other things that would put you a little out of your comfort zone but satisfy some sort of need? Refer back, or add these things to your "Wouldn't it be cool if…" list. Who knows, one of these options could be part of your adventure in Part Two.

Lastly, here is a little more self reflection.

- What has been holding you back from participating in these new experiences that you are interested in?

  ▷ Are you feeling this way because you are always stuck around the same people? Or are you expected to behave a certain way?

  ▷ What would life look like if you freed yourself from those restrictions?

I know these are some heavy, challenging questions. So do your best to answer honestly and without judgment. This is all part of figuring out who you are right now and where your fairytale is really pulling you to head in the future.

You consider what the barkeep shared with you, chewing a large bite of chicken in your mouth. "I've been considering putting together a traveling party."

The barkeep smiles at you. "That so? What are you hunting?"

"Anything that will take me farther," you pause. "North."

The barkeep laughs. "Sounds like your crew, Orik. Got room for another?"

The dwarf turns to you fully. He studies you from head to toe. You try not to squirm under his shrewd gaze. "Aye, we're headed north. Got a few gigs along the way. Guess it wouldn't hurt to split it with one more."

"Who's your crew?" You ask, looking out over the rest of the tavern.

"Got a few of us. They're wrapped up in the fights. Wait around and when things die down, I'll introduce ya."

LEVEL EIGHT - NPCS

The Power of Weak Ties

"People live through their interactions
with one another! It's because of all the
people that I am what I am today."

FROM MARIE ADLAI IN PIERROT'S BLACK
CLOVER ANIMATED TV SERIES

Several hours pass and you eat and drink your fill, chatting with the dwarf and the barkeep and the other patrons who cycle in and out throughout the night as the fights continue. Eventually, the healer from the apothecary comes in and sits beside the dwarf, ordering a pint. You are surprised to see him wrap his arm around her. You try to make yourself a little scarce when they start to kiss.

The barkeep notices your discomfort, slides you another drink, and gestures for you to go back and watch the last of the fights. "Don't worry," he whispers. "They're only like this for ten minutes or so." He smirks. You acquiesce and carry your pint back over to the fighting pits.

You watch the fights from the back, the edge of the circle, but honestly the idea of people punching each other to unconsciousness is not what you would consider your favorite entertainment. Though, you cannot deny there is a spirit about this place.

When the fights finish up for the night and the pit is hidden by the floorboards again and the tables shifted back into position, the dwarf waves you toward a corner of the room. A group has pushed three circular tables together. They are laughing and drinking, but they pause to welcome you as the dwarf introduces you.

He begins with the human healer from the apothecary. "This is my wife, Lila."

"We met earlier today." Lila nods as she shakes your hand.

"She lives here in town and works her shop, but occasionally she travels along with us to gather ingredients."

Lila laughs and places her arms around his shoulders, resting her head on top of his. "Or I hire them to go get the ingredients I have no desire of scrounging up on my own."

The dwarf continues, pointing toward the pair of scrawny boys who had hopped into the pit earlier. Now that they are up close, they appear to be twins. "Serge and Marx. No, they're not twins, but damn do they look it. They're headed south for us tomorrow. Got a shipment coming in. They're going to pick it up."

"Where south? I just came up from that way."

Serge raises his eyebrows at you. "You do have the look of a southerner."

Marx slaps him on the arm. "Ah, shut up."

"More than a few towns over," Serge says. "It will probably take us a week to get there."

The dwarf waves them off and moves down the table. "It's Jonathan and Nemirah you'll be pleased to meet. They are traveling north with me at the end of the week." He turns to his friends. "We got ourselves a fourth."

Nemirah shakes your hand and gestures for you to take the seat beside her.

Jonathan leans across the table toward you. "Why are you headed north?"

You sigh. "I guess I am not sure yet, just figuring it out. Figuring myself out. But I need to pave my way and could use the protection of a group on the road. And the money—"

"You're speaking to the choir."

Lila includes, "I am stocking the others up with materials at the shop tomorrow. Come by, I will make sure you are outfitted for your travels."

"Are you sure? I would never want to impose."

"If you are going to be protecting Orik's back, I want to make sure you have everything you need."

Yes, there is definitely a certain spirit about this place and these people. You almost feel connected to them already, though you barely know them. Somehow you feel like you have been supported more by them than by some people you might have called friends since childhood.

It is an odd sensation building in your chest. You feel a genuine warmth and a desire to be of service to these people, and also a little regret that other people in your life did not live up to this sort of physical emotion.

Even if you are lost, Orik and his crew are going to guide you to the next step forward. You have no idea whether it's going to be the right step or not, but they are opening doors of opportunity for you. You make a decision. You plan to not only appreciate it, but embrace it to the fullest.

Here is just a little scientific insight on the power of weak ties before we go any further.

According to an article in the Stanford Report from September 15th, 2022, a team of Stanford, MIT, and Harvard scientists found "weaker ties" are more beneficial for job seekers. In a quote from the article, "Brynjolfsson co-led the first large-scale, longitudinal, experimental study on the 'strength of weak ties,' one of the most influential social theories of the last 100 years. The 'strength of weak ties' theory maintains that infrequent, arm's length relationships - known as weak ties - are more beneficial for employment opportunities, promotions, and wages than strong ties…The team's findings are detailed in a paper, titled *A causal test of the strength of weak ties* that was published in the journal *Science*."

When I first learned about the power of weak ties, it was like a lightbulb of appreciation going off in my head. When we are asked who we are grateful for, we often think of those closest to us. Our parents, our partners, our siblings, or best friends. Yes, while these strong ties are integral to us on a day-to-day basis, we often forget about the power our weak ties sometimes have on changing the trajectory of our lives, whether in a very obvious or completely subconscious way. Not only that, but we forget to be grateful for them.

Sometimes our friends and family cannot see the change we seek to enact in ourselves. They see who we were years ago when we first met them, where we currently are, not always where we could be. It takes leaning into weak ties to propel us forward.

People I have barely met invited me to their movie premieres where I met amazing industry connections. A friend of a sister of my friend helped me train my very difficult rescue dog.

It was a sales manager at my first job who wrote a glowing review for me on LinkedIn that helped me get my next job when I got furloughed during the pandemic.

It was the husband of a coworker who took the time out of his busy schedule to talk with me over the phone about attending DePaul University like he had and pursuing becoming a screenwriter.

It was a thesis professor who I had spent less than ten weeks with who encouraged another professor to hire me as a graduate assistant, not only giving me valuable job experience in script development, but a needed monetary stipend and tuition waiver that helped make paying for my graduate school experience just a little more affordable.

These are just a few of my weak ties, and I am so grateful for them and the impact they have made on my life.

When you think about it, your weak ties are kind of like the NPCs, or non-player characters, in your campaign. They are the people you meet who give you helpful advice or needed information. They correct your course or set you on to a new destination. If you are anything like us in our campaign, we tend to collect them. Our NPCs become our cherished friends. We keep pulling them back into the narrative. Keep trusting them. We drive our DM wild because she has to play so many characters.

In the end, these characters can become friends and trusted acquaintances. In our minds, it would be rude to shove them aside or forget the impact they have made.

You never know who will share your name in the right room.

SESSION RECAP:

We are going to take a moment to reflect again before we start on our side quest. So, open up your journal, head to a fresh page, and start to think.

Who are those people who came into your life either for a moment or for a long time and were there to help you make your biggest decisions? Again, try to not think of those people who are entrenched in your life, your strong ties, but rather those people who appear, make an impact, and fade back into the background again.

Who are those people who gave you advice that you took to heart?

Did anyone change the direction or trajectory of your life for the better despite having nothing to gain from the experience themselves?

These people could be teachers, professors, bosses, employers, an elder sibling of a friend, a counselor, a nurse, a therapist, a librarian, or any number of people in between.

Make a list of them.

Write their names down and a brief statement of what they did for you.

When you have completed your list to the best of your ability, write this line at the bottom of the page.

"I am grateful for the impact my weak ties have had on my life."

When searching for miracles, when searching for the next amazing opportunity, it is important to come from a place of gratitude. So, now it's time to thank those who have gotten you this far, gotten you to this moment, so that you might begin a new adventure.

SIDE QUEST:

The first side quest in this section is to keep that gratitude flowing. You have a list of people now who have made an impact on your life. Reach out to them. Whether it is an email, a text, a call, or a LinkedIn DM, shoot them a quick message. Let them know how grateful you are for their small act of kindness. If you would like, let them know where you are because of it. These people will be amazed to hear how an act they have likely forgotten about has shaped the life of another human in such a way.

Now on to step two. This one is not immediate, but keep your eyes and ears open for moments when you can pass along this kindness that you received to someone else. Do you have the opportunity to recommend a coworker for a promotion? Can you help an intern get their foot in the door in your industry? Can you offer to help someone with their resume? Can you support the inspiration of a child to pursue a big passion?

These opportunities are going to suddenly appear all around you and all the time. As you step into the spirit of adventure and pursue big dreams, the best thing you can do is pass the baton along. Grab hands and pull people up to join you. One day, you are going to be the weak tie that they reach out to. So be open and be prepared. You don't have to go searching. You just have to answer when the time comes to you.

In the *Throne of Glass* series by Sarah J. Maas, the protagonist moved through life with kindness toward others. She helped people even when there was no reward for herself. When her dark moment came and she suddenly needed to call for aid, they showed up for her.

Kindness matters. Kindness matters in the smallest moments of life, so hold that close as you move forward in the adventure.

"Got any special skills?" Orik asks you.

"Um." You had not thought about this one. "I'm a skilled speaker. Negotiator." The looks at the table aren't dull, but they certainly aren't impressed. You fumble. "No, I mean it. It's got a price, I can negotiate it."

You hear a chuckle behind you. It's the barkeep. "That they can," he says. "Got three nights and meals from me for nine. I will never live it down."

The others at the table laugh heartily.

"What about weapons?" Orik asks you. "You seem to know the road is dangerous. Some of the quarries we're after are not the tamest of beasts."

"I can handle myself with a knife," you quickly assure him.

The table nods.

Nemirah quickly unsheathes and spins a knife holstered at her waist. It deftly curls through her fingers. "Me too."

You blush with embarrassment. "Looks like you might be a bit more advanced than me."

Nemirah smiles. "I would be happy to teach you."

Again, you are surprised by the assistance and kindness of these people. "That sounds like a plan."

"Great. Out back behind the apothecary when we go pick up our supplies. They got some targets set up in the little yard out back."

You cannot help but smile.

You get lost in the talking, drinking, and camaraderie. By the time you make it back to your room, you can't even call it evening anymore. It is probably hinting toward early morning. You shut the shutters and go to sleep, burying your face in the pillow a few hours later when the sun wakes you up and shines through the slats.

You give yourself a few hours to just be lazy and lounge, but you can't sleep.

Eventually you give in and head downstairs for breakfast. You don't know how the barkeep does it, but he is back again. He is as lively and chipper as ever. You wonder how much sleep he operates on, but he runs a tight ship and this place appears to be his pride and joy. There is certainly a lot that can be said for something simple feeling so right.

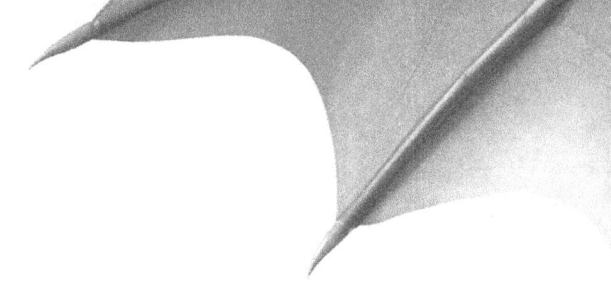

LEVEL NINE - MENTOR

A Guide Beyond Measure

"All mentors have a way of seeing more of our faults than we would like, it's the only way we grow."

FROM PADMÉ AMIDALA IN GEORGE LUCAS' STAR
WARS: EPISODE II: ATTACK OF THE CLONES

With food in your belly and a plan for the day, you almost have a skip in your step as you head down the road to the apothecary. You have made sure to don clothes that are loose and fluid. You have even polished up your belt and your knife. With the prospect of learning from a real expert, you are suddenly taking pride in what skill you already have. You brushed up on some technique in the mirror before departing your room.

You reach the apothecary and step inside first. The same workers are there again today. Lila looks up as you enter. "You are the first to make it!" she says cheerily.

You laugh. "It's nearly midday."

"Let's just say Orik's crew is a bunch of hardworking buggers when they are on the road. But give 'em some drinks and some peace and they are a bunch of wastrels."

"Who are you calling a wastrel?" Jonathan calls as he swings the door open. He saunters into the room like he is a part of some great dance. He sways from shelf to shelf, peering and picking various items into his arms.

"Ah, ah, ah," Lila argues. "I told you I was stocking you up. Not letting you rob the place."

"This *is* my share of the stock," Jonathan argues.

The other young woman behind the counter giggles and covers her mouth with her hand. Jonathan clocks it and saunters over to her. You are starting to tell this is a normal occurrence and perhaps a regular flirtation. "Gracie, darling. You will convince her, won't you?"

Lila frowns. "Of course Grace wouldn't dare to allow our inventory to go missing."

"Of course not, Miss Brannockburn."

Lila laughs and pats Grace on the shoulder. "I'm mostly kidding, my dear."

"So." Jonathan leans against the counter. He bats his eyelashes persuasively. "What can I have?"

Lila considers him and the wares he has set on the counter carefully. "You can take those two potions." She gestures over to you. "Give those other two to your new companion." She shuffles into the back room where the old man is working again, apologizing as she squeezes by him. "Sorry, Pa. Did you see where I put the dried meat?"

The older man points without speaking and Lila comes back with a crate. "I got two weeks' worth of dried rations for the lot of you."

Jonathan smacks his lips, but not in a way that you assume he enjoys this. It rather feels like sick disappointment. "Just what I want for two weeks, dried cow lard."

Grace shakes her head. "It's not lard. She bought the meat straight from the butcher and prepared it herself."

Lila waves Grace's defense away. "He knows that. He just has no appreciation for my skills." She snatches a bag of dried rations and tosses it across the room to you. "Hide that among your own things, or you may find that your share slowly disappears."

Jonathan is already lifting the crate. "Ah, come on. You know I don't like 'em."

"So why do you eat them?"

"Perhaps if they were pork instead."

"You *are* a pig," another voice speaks from the door as the chime rings again. You turn to see Nemirah enter the apothecary and walk to the group. Lila slips her a few small items from the other side of the counter which Nemirah pockets. Her hands snatch another portioned bag from the crate as well. "Rations for me, thank you."

Jonathan waves her away as he turns to exit. "I will load these up on the cart, make sure they are all locked up and secured."

As he disappears, Nemirah turns to you. "Are you ready for some lessons?"

You nod in excitement as she leads you behind the counter, scooching by the kind old man who stands up off his stool to allow you to pass, and out into the yard beyond. It is not very big and is surrounded by a short fence that maybe reaches up to your thigh. Among a garden of various herbs and vegetables and flowers, a few targets are set up at various distances.

Nemirah tosses her knife up and down in her hand absentmindedly. "Now, why don't you start with just a few throws of your own so I can see what I am working with?"

You are suddenly self-conscious. You take a few breaths and move to the center of the yard. Your hands sweat a little, but you shake yourself to ease the jitters and focus.

You throw your knife at the nearest target. A sigh of relief. You hit the target, and not only that but nearly the edge of the inner ring. Nemirah just nods as she walks to your knife and pulls it out of the target. She hands it to you. "That one now," she says as she gestures to the farther target.

With a little bit of confidence restored, you aim and huck your knife at the middle distance target. You make the throw again, but this time the knife sits poised more toward the outer edge of the target. You are expecting a critique, but Nemirah merely nods again and retrieves your knife for you.

"And the farthest one," she instructs.

You take your knife back and consider the target. That is definitely farther than you have ever attempted to throw. You lift your arm and fling with all of your might. To your embarrassment, it sails far above the target, clatters against the wooden fence of the apothecary, and tumbles directly to the ground. You rush to go grab it before Nemirah does it for you.

As you pick it up, you meet her gaze. She just gestures for you to return to the spot where you were standing and try again.

"This time," she says as you reach your place, "don't just throw with your arm. Step with your feet into it."

You nod, trying to walk through what that would look like in your mind. You face the target again. Stepping forward, you release with the momentum of your body behind it. Your knife sails forward and strikes the target.

Unfortunately, it's the handle end, not the point, and it clatters to the dirt.

"Good." Nemirah smiles. "Again."

The importance of a mentor's role in each person's personal journey is quite clear in many of our favorite stories. Finding the right mentor can be the difference between success and failure. It does not matter how active that mentor was in the story, even just being able to bounce ideas back and forth can be a big help.

Here are just a few of my favorite helpful, if sometimes frustrating, mentors:

- Yoda & Luke Skywalker

- Mr. Miyagi & The Karate Kid

- Gandalf & The entire Fellowship of the Ring

- Sean Maguire & Will Hunting

- Halt O'Carrick & Will Treaty

- Aslan & The Pevensie Children

- Rafiki & Simba

- Haymitch Abernathy & Katniss Everdeen

Can you think of any more? 100% you can at least think of one from all of your favorite stories.

Growing up, I don't think I ever considered becoming a professional writer until the idea was planted in my head by my freshman year English teacher. On one of my assignments he wrote,

"You're writing a book? I want to read it." Even though it took many years to realize it, I never forgot this simple phrase that he said. We all have those amazing teachers who engrain in us some of our most impactful school memories. I am grateful to have kept in close contact so that inspiration never left me. To this day, he cheers me on and reads some of my drafts. I know that he's proud of the passion I have developed for the craft even if I never chose to become published. However, it feels really good to show him his time wasn't wasted.

Who are the other available mentors in your life so far? A teacher? A professor? A coach? Your boss? Maybe even a friend's parent or a great colleague at work?

Frankly, you can have many mentors! Surround yourself with them and you will be much better off for it.

SESSION RECAP:

Now I know you probably already have some ideas of who your past mentors have been, but as we look ahead to Part Two of this book, you don't yet know what your next adventure will be or who is going to step into the role of mentor in your life. While that unknown can be frightening, it can also be kind of exciting. Who is going to be that person you are looking up to? Who is guiding you? Who is sharing this adventure and celebrating your success?

Sometimes the best mentors are the ones who are found when and where we least expect them. As we work through this exercise, I don't want you to limit yourself, rather utilize this as a starting point. As your self-awareness grows, you will begin to recognize new mentors that don't fit what you lay out here in this session recap portion of the chapter. However, I think this is a key place to start.

Time to jot and journal. Don't get into specifics. We are speaking in generalities. Eventually, we are going to ask questions like who do I know that is already doing what I want to do? But for now, since we haven't decided on the next fairytale yet, focus instead on how this person might make you feel. How do they behave? How do they support you? What are you looking for? Nothing is set in stone. Rather, think about your own personality and what you would prefer when it comes to finding a mentor.

- Where are you going to find the mentor to your fairytale? Do you want to communicate with them online? Or would you rather meet them in person?

- What does your mentor bring to the table? Are they a complete expert? Or are they someone who is just a few steps ahead of you?

- Are they strict and tough to put you in some sort of order? Or are they kind and supportive, always inspiring you?

- Is this a person from your past (who you're already comfortable with) who has always cheered you on whenever you pursued a new endeavor? Or is this someone you haven't met yet, because expanding your circle might be pretty key to your journey?

In a way, writing this out will make it easier to find them because you'll "know 'em when you see 'em."

When I wrote down what I was looking for in a partner, super specifically, it made it easy to pass on tempting options that were not checking all the boxes. When I found my partner, it made it easy to say yes and commit.

So, yes, let's say we are manifesting the right mentor, because as we mentioned above, the right mentor can make or break you along the road of the journey.

SIDE QUEST:

Things are going to start kicking into gear as we head into Part Two, so now is the time to take a breather. Let's watch a movie!

Think back to movies you haven't watched in a while. Think back to movies you loved as a kid or as a teenager. What story has an amazing mentor character? We're watching specifically for that. Don't watch a new movie. Don't watch a movie you have never seen before. You need to pick something that is familiar and comforting. Do you know all the words to the movie? Even better!

The more you become aware of the role of mentors in the lives of characters, the more you will begin to see where mentors begin to step into your own life. You may even notice people that you have, up until this moment, overlooked, that you now realize act as a mentor figure in your life.

So, go pop some popcorn and spend two to three hours getting lost in an amazing story. After all, great stories can not only provide us entertainment and relief, but the courage to keep pushing through.

You are sweating profusely when Nemirah hands you a waterskin and gestures for you to sit down. Now that it is afternoon, the apothecary building is shading the little garden from the falling sun. You drink and breathe deeply. That was some of the most taxing work you had done physically training with a knife…literally ever. You had never concentrated on it for so long before. Luckily, you made significant progress.

Nemirah was definitely a tough tutor, but she did not make you feel like a fool. Instead you felt yourself inspired, learning not just from the words she said but the demonstrations she showed. As you sit there beside each other, you know you are eager to learn more, but you are not sure if your body will hold up to the vigorous physical activity just yet.

Nemirah takes the waterskin back from you and drinks as well. "You are skilled with a knife, so long as we keep you at a mid-range distance. We have yet to see how you will do up close, but I guess that all comes with time."

"Will I have to do that? Fight up close?"

"I guess it all depends. If we are out in the wild hunting animals, the likelihood of having some space increases. But as we near the northern towns, our bounties and jobs may move a bit more indoors."

"That sounds like it would require some finesse."

"Yes, some."

"Where did you learn your knife skills?"

"I had a teacher, too. A great teacher." Nemirah stares off wistfully at the sky. "It takes a special sort of person, but when you find them, they have the power to transform your life. They instill this will to succeed in you that you never had before. At least for me, I want to do nothing more than make them proud."

"I am sure your teacher is already very proud of you."

Nemirah nods. "Yes, I would like to hope so."

Mindset: Your Closest Friend or Greatest Foe

"I'm the rock against which the surf crashes. Nothing can break me."

FROM NESTA ARCHERON IN SARAH J
MAAS' A COURT OF SILVER FLAMES

You return to the inn in the evening, enjoy another hot meal courtesy of the barkeep, and turn to head upstairs. Some of Orik's crew waves you over. They already have cards splayed out on the table between them. Tankards poised to be drunk.

You wander over. "Actually I'm going to head up for the night. A hot bath is calling my name."

Marx laughs. "Sounds like a plan. Who knows when the next chance you'll get will be, eh?"

You nod. This thought had not crossed your mind, but he's right.

You bid the group goodnight and move upstairs.

There is a communal bathing chamber on your floor. You head inside and lock the door behind you, asserting your claim on the space for the next hour or so.

At first, you stand there, hovering over the tub. You look around. How does this work? Until you touch the edge of the tub and it begins to fill with hot, steamy water, a fragrance on the air as soap bubbles appear at the surface. Pure magic. You had thought this was just your standard roadside tavern, but clearly the barkeep has a little something up his sleeve.

You shed your clothes and settle into the water when the tub is filled completely.

Ahhhh. You sigh, submerging yourself all the way to the neck.

You sink a little further. The water covers your ears and dashes out the sound of the tavern below. In the quiet, you have a real moment of peace. That is, until your mind speaks up and begins to race, taking over the silence. God forbid you have a moment of complete quiet.

You try to push the thoughts back and shove them down, but you know it's no use. Your thoughts are your constant companion. You have lived with this voice for your entire life. You will continue to live with it into your old age.

Tired, you don't have the current will to try to control it, so you let the thoughts run and race where they please.

It all begins anew tomorrow, they tell you. You have no idea where the road will take you, what monsters you will face, or what decisions you will have to make. Your hands start to shake a little bit as you almost let those thoughts start to overwhelm you.

It is scary and daunting, stepping out onto the road.

What are you going to do? Are the choices you make going to be right? What if you fail? What if it's not what you expected?

On and on the thoughts circle.

You push your head up out of the water. No, no, no. This will not do.

The tavern din below returns and the sounds help to quiet some of your thoughts and send them rippling to the background. You focus on the sensation of the hot water comforting your body on all sides. You take a deep breath in, remembering to enjoy the delightful scent of the magical soap bubbles. In. Out. You start to count your breaths. You glance at the shining, rainbow reflections on the surface of the bubbles themselves.

Then, those thoughts start to quiet. Settle.

Your thoughts have all the right to be there. What you are doing is so different, so crazy, so vastly departed from your norm, that there are hundreds of questions. However, 99% of them you don't have the answer to. You can only speculate.

You decide you are not going to let the anxious fears dictate your decisions. You are going to start trusting your gut and your brain together, in tandem, but not that wild voice inside your head because it will say anything to get attention. One moment it might agree with you, the next it's arguing. You try to remind yourself that your thoughts are but clouds in the sky of your mind. So you try to observe them and let them pass until the bath water turns chilly around you and your fingers start to prune.

As you travel through life, the only companion you have <u>at all times</u> and <u>in all places</u> is your own mind. The people in our lives come in and out. Sometimes they leave us. Some even leave us "halfway through the wood." Even our favorite characters meet us somewhere along the road. No one knows your full journey.

Only you and the consciousness that speaks to you inside your head.

Your mindset is going to be your closest friend or greatest foe, because it is the only thing truly riding alongside you at all hours of the day. So it's imperative that you take the time to align with it, to lay down the rules, and set before yourself a plan if the voice tries to deter you later on. Time to set boundaries!

There is a great benefit to having positivity and optimism as you move forward. Because what do we know? We lack control. We cannot control what the world will do to us, what will be thrown our way. What we *can* control is how we react. We can throw in the towel, kick and scream, or we can keep fighting for our fairytale.

Let me say right now that as you choose your adventure and step out on the road, it's going to be EASY at some point to give up. All the decisions you make are going to be hard, because you are going to have to put something long term before other things that might bring you quick pleasure. We are warriors fighting for the chance of long-term happiness over giving in to short-term gratification.

As a writer, I can tell you I have had my fair share of fighting with my own mind. It comes to me in the form of imposter syndrome where I say to myself every single nasty thing that you would be appalled at if someone said it to you in person. Your writing sucks. You can't get the plot right. No one is going to read that story. Your editors and early readers are lying to you about how they enjoyed it. They just didn't want to hurt your feelings. What happens when you fail? You think this story is going to make it as a Blockbuster movie?

Over time, my imposter syndrome and I have found our symbiosis, if only because I listen to it just enough to keep me attentive and conscious to all my choices, but not enough where I become down and throw in the towel.

If you are already battling with your mind, I promise that you are going to overcome it. You've come to the right place and can find a way through. It will take time, but eventually that voice in your head will fall in line once you lay down the rules. It's your life. You're in charge. That voice is just along for the ride.

So say it with me: "I will not allow myself, my mindset, to become my enemy." There are enough "enemies" in the world as is.

Having cancer in your mid-twenties, you have every RIGHT to be upset, down, depressed, and angry. There is not a single person who wouldn't GET IT, but you know what wouldn't serve me in the end? That negativity.

Why should I give in to anger? Live in anger? Act selfishly? Hurt those around me? All because I am in pain? If I was mean to my nurses, they sure as hell wouldn't have been so thoughtful. They wouldn't have gone out of their way to make me extra comfortable, bring me snacks, or add my name to a list of potential financial assistance recipients.

If I was mean to my mother or my partner, they would have cared for me, but not dropped what they were doing to be by my side through it all.

If I had given in to being cranky at work, I would not have gained the same love and respect from my coworkers and clients that I now enjoy.

Positivity served me much better.

Being open, being kind, and sharing my story—staying determined to continue with positivity every step of the way—made cancer a blip rather than a persona. I am not cancer. I beat cancer. I am the cancer *warrior*.

I feel the same about any fight you are fighting. Don't let the trouble make you hard or make you cruel. Whether you are facing off against a disease, a system, an unfair piece of blame — don't let the world turn you mean. Instead, fight with determination and fight with grace. Help us build a better world that is kind and just and full of healing. Hurt people tend to hurt people, but we are going to show that stereotype who's boss.

If you are in the dark, there is always a way out. Find your guiding light.

If you slip into depression, fear, and anger in response to the difficulties in your life, don't criticise yourself. We all will slip back into darkness sometimes. Once you recognize when you are being drawn back to the shadows, reconnect with your fairytale. The path is still there to find and start walking on again.

There were a lot of days when I had to turn to Leona in the silence of night, crying in my pillow, for her to redirect the movement of my thoughts and emotions. That is why I had her. That is why I trust her to this day. She was my reminder in the broken moments that no matter what happens, there is always a path to healing and redemption.

Your character is going to be the same.

Because now, in pursuit of your new adventure, if you fail one day or give up for a period of time, you aren't going to beat yourself up. You are going to remember that you are no longer on square one. The actions you did accomplish have brought you further, and now you are just at a redirection point. The choice to maintain that perspective is going to mean a lot.

Danika Fendyr's main quote from *House of Earth and Blood* by Sarah J. Maas was "Through love all is possible." It is now that we build great love. Not for a person or a concept, just for ourselves. Have great love for yourself. Enjoy this process. Be eager for all the ups and downs of this journey you are about to embark on because that means you're moving. No matter what, you are going to learn something. And to me, that's pretty awesome.

SESSION RECAP:

Now, this side quest may seem a bit crazy, and I will admit it—I am a bit crazy. When you face off with an enemy like cancer before you hit the age of thirty, it knocks you a bit out of stride and maybe off your rocker. Though, I feel it was in a good way.

Honestly, this is the nuts and bolts of what this book is all about, so run with me.

Leona was my rock throughout my cancer journey. I talked to her and trusted her like a child would talk to and trust their imaginary friend. Each morning, I would wake up and roll my twenty-sided dice. If the number was low, it was Leona telling me to take it easy that day. If the number was high, it was her kick in my butt to push ahead into the day because I had nothing to lose. It felt good when the rest of life was a mess to check in with her each day and know that she walked beside me. It was incredibly grounding. Even now, years beyond, I still roll. It's a comfort and a reminder that I never walk alone. She walks beside me because warriors walk together.

So, it's time for you to invite your comfort character or characters to walk alongside you. You are about to step out on the road of your new journey. So, flip back to your notes from Level Three. Who were the characters that you look up to, who do you wish you could be more like, and who inspires you?

Sit and imagine them in the room with you.

Tell them you are about to step out on the road and pursue your next big adventure and that you will need their support. Get a sense of their reaction. Is it their personality type to draw back and question you about the nature of such a journey? Or are they already jumping up saying hell yeah?

Welcome them close.

Next, from the room of adventurers, select the one who is going to be your main companion and your guide. They don't have to be the one you move with forever, but who is the one that inspires you most right now? Whose energy do you need?

If you are up for a bit of journaling, open to the next page and write this character a letter, like you are going to send it to them inviting them on an adventure. It could be like the contract the dwarves mock up for Bilbo in The Hobbit. Or it could be a quick, friendly, "Hey, meet me at the tavern at 6 pm. We're planning an adventure!"

How would you invite this character to join your party and journey with you? What skills do they have that you need? What do you feel you have to offer them? Is there going to be excitement? Adventure? Reward?

Make the offer enticing! Because your life and your dreams certainly are going to be!

Mindset can be one of the most challenging things to get a handle on. If you are prone to talking down to yourself, have depression, or generally have trouble keeping positive, I have another book for you for further reading after you finish this book! The Untethered Soul: The Journey Beyond Yourself by Michael Alan Singer. I will add it to the suggested future reading list at the end of this book. Honestly, I think it is great for everyone to start to get familiar with their own internal voice.

It made me think about my mind in a different way and get a sense of the difference between my consciousness resting at the seat of my personhood and the loud voice that always wants to talk and get its way.

SIDE QUEST:

Now that you have invited your comfort or inspiration character to walk alongside you, it is time to set yourself up for success. Because on the hard days, this needs to be accessible and easy to see. You are going to need constant reminders.

So, find a really cool picture of this character and set it as the background on your phone or computer, somewhere you will see it often. Or, you can print it out and hang it on your fridge, above your desk, or beside your bed. Whenever you see them, they will remind you of your journey. It will be a subtle reminder, a push to keep going. Because frankly…they would.

If you would like to get a little deeper with your character each day, it's time to implement your "rolling habit." If you have a twenty-sided dice or d20, set your dice somewhere you will see it each morning— next to your bed or beside your jewelry box. If you don't have a d20, there are great online sites you can use instead. You can literally Google 'online d20 roller' and one pops up immediately! You just have to click: roll. If you are going the digital route, keep that as an open tab on your search app.

You can roll each day and think of it like your character telling you what you need for the day. I like to think...

- 01 - Warning! Today you need to guard your heart and your soul. Do everything you can to protect yourself and don't make ANY big decisions.

- 02 through 05 - Do what you have to do, then take it easy. Take a break. Watch a show. Pull off the gas pedal for a second. We don't need to go anywhere fast.

- 06 through 10 - Focus on the grounding that comes through stable habits. Try to do what you have to do, particularly focusing on the healthy habits that are going to keep you going like eating, drinking water, or going for a walk.

- 11 through 15 - Life's hitting its stride. Keep working at your goals and habits. Push yourself to go a little further. Instead of just a walk, try a run-walk or get a workout in at the gym. Spend a few extra minutes training your dog. Write 100 more words.

- 16 through 19 - Take advantage! We're in such a great spot, so go after your goals. Positivity is your outlook, because I'm on your side. It's gonna be a good day!

- 20 - Tackle something huge today! Take a big risk! Big rewards are coming! Trust in the amazingness of this day and open your eyes to an opportunity you might otherwise miss!

Do those suggestions make you feel good? You will note that not a single line tells you to throw in the towel or give up. Even rolling a '1' isn't the end of the world. Rather, we need to remind ourselves to rest and take our foot off the gas pedal when things are getting challenging—because even without gas, a car in motion, stays in motion.

That's it for now!

Don't worry, we will be back touching base with your character very soon.

As you step out of the tub and wrap a comfy, soft towel around your body, your determination settles. You remember that you are not on your own anymore. You will have a group of people you will travel alongside. Though each of your goals are different in the end, it is inspiring to know that they walk the path with you.

You catch this feeling that you are EXACTLY where you were always meant to be. You make the decision to believe it in this moment, and you have never felt better.

The night is getting late. You step into bed and blow out your candle. The sooner you sleep, the sooner you can rise to the light of the new day and learn all that it has to offer you.

PART TWO

The Pursuit of Adventure

A Purpose in Mind & Moving Forward

"I'm going on an adventure!"

From Bilbo Baggins in J.R.R.
Tolkien's The Hobbit

You are not surprised to find that you and Nemirah are the first downstairs in the morning. There is no sign of Orik or Jonathan. Last night you had left the boys drinking and gambling, so no doubt they would be slow moving when rising this morning.

Accepting your last breakfast from the tavern keeper, you exchange him for the key to your room. You have repacked all of your belongings in your pack, completely prepared to set out. At least physically.

Unfortunately, your nerves are 100% on edge. Your fingers twitch with a fidgeting energy. Nemirah smiles as she settles down across from you with her warm bowl of porridge. She gestures to your hand that shakes even as you spoon the sugary warmth into your mouth. "Pre-adventure jitters?"

"I've never done anything like this before."

Nemirah considers you thoughtfully. "Then how did you get here?"

You consider her question and then realize she is smirking at you. She already knows the answer to her own question. She just wants to make you realize it.

"I guess," you begin, testing the words in your mouth before you share them, "I've never headed out with a crew."

"Let me say it's better than going out alone."

"Or anything so dangerous."

"When you're with a crew, nothing is as dangerous to weather as it might be alone."

You can't help but nod in agreement.

You fall into companionable silence and when you're both almost finished eating, Orik and Jonathan make their noisy entrance to the tavern, both from outside on the street. No doubt Orik was saying his last good-byes to Lila. Jonathan was the one who was supposed to be in charge of your cart, so he was probably in the stables getting the horses ready.

Orik slaps a hand on either hip and considers the table. "Done with your morning rituals?"

Nemirah snorts. "We've been waiting for you to show."

Orik grunts, but the dark bags under his eyes betray him. He waves Nemirah's comment off. "Did you each pull your bounties?"

Nemirah nods, but you look at Orik quizzically. "I thought we were all headed out together. On the same bounty."

Jonathan presses closer to you. His hands rest on your shoulders and spin you around to the barkeep's board of parchment. "We do, but we each grab our own, too. Take turns getting them done along the way for extra coin."

Orik smiles. "Go on, pick something along the way to Kahln."

You stumble over toward the board. Nemirah and Jonathan join you, eager to offer their advice and commentary. You carefully read all the papers, considering your options.

"We could definitely do the monster hunting," Jonathan recommends. "You think that's 500 gold each?"

"That sounds…dangerous," you answer. "What about helping the poor guy move? We're on our way to Kahln anyway. We can hit it when we get there."

Nemirah snorts. "For ale and turkey legs. I could get that on my own without doing any work."

"Then what about the cow? That sounds nice!"

Jonathan rubs the back of his neck. "I'm just saying that sounds boring."

You glance between the two of them with frustration, but both just shrug their shoulders. This is YOUR bounty after all.

There is a quote from Alexander Den Heijer I love that says, "You often feel tired not because you have done too much, but because you've done too little of what sparks a light in you."

As someone living and working in the present day, I really think it's both. To make ends meet, we might have to work two jobs, stay up late doing homework to get it done after the kids go to sleep, or take on all the house chores because your partner has a busy season at work. At the same time, with all these to-dos, commitments, and expectations, we don't have much time, if any, to do what brings us joy.

Now's the time to change that. We are going to prioritize a little bit of joy. You have made it this far, it is time to pick <u>an adventure</u> that will spark a little light in you.

Now this is very, very important. We are going to start SMALL. This isn't the time to tackle your biggest dream or goal. If you are pouting right now, I'm sorry, but I promise we will get there in due time. You trusted me so far. Keep trusting.

This is going to be a tiny goal just for you. Think of it like your own personal side quest! We will call it the everyday fairytale. If you are working through this book with a friend or partner, you are both going to pick different personal goals to pursue separately (yes, just like Jonathan and Nemirah pulled their own bounties from the tavern wall separate from yours).

There will be time to come back later and plan a joint goal as well.

This little bounty you pluck from your board is a task you can comfortably complete in a month or maybe two. To quote every other goal setting book ever: make it Specific, Measurable, Achievable, Relevant, and Time Bound. Aka S.M.A.R.T.

If you have a ton of ideas, maybe you want to make your own bounty board of post-it notes and select one at random!

I am going to provide a few examples just to get your mind working, again these might be a bit specific to me. Don't come for me! Before you decide completely, make sure you complete the session recap portion of this chapter. I will be walking you through a few writing prompts that may help you decide what your first adventure is going to be.

Ideas of side quests I might choose:

- Write one handwritten letter to a different friend every week for the next two months

- Go to the gym and use the stair climber twice a week for four weeks for at least ten minutes

- Save $100 toward a special birthday gift for my partner in the next four weeks by selling a few items I don't want anymore on Facebook marketplace

- Finish the page on my website for my developmental editing services in four weeks so I can begin to attract clients

- Visit the local library and check out a new book, audiobook, movie, or CD once per week for two months

You see how all of my examples set a strong timeframe as well as bite-sized goals that are achievable if I set my mind to it? This everyday fairytale can be completely fun or it can challenge you toward a bigger, more serious self development goal.

The biggest thing is to make sure that it inspires you, that it's something you really want, and working toward it would make you happy.

Over the next few chapters we are going to discuss laying out a plan to achieve your everyday fairytale as well as a reward system to help you take the steps along the way. For now though, let's focus on hammering out our first tiny adventure.

SESSION RECAP:

Open up your journal and answer the following questions to help you home in on your everyday fairytale!

1. What do you want to be known for? What is the first step toward being known for that?
2. Are there any skills that you have that you would like to develop further?
3. Are there any skills that you DON'T have that you would like to start to develop?

4. What project has been weighing on your mind that you have been putting off lately?

Some of the questions here should set off the neon lights like "Hello hello—here it is!" But if not, you may want to return to your "Wouldn't it be cool if…" list to get some more inspiration.

SIDE QUEST:

This is the part I am particularly excited about. My request is that you decide on your everyday fairytale and email it to me.

Yes, I am giving you my real email: connect@colleenochab.com

Title the subject line: FFYF Everyday Fairytale

I am going to do my best to respond to every single one.

As this community grows and all of us are fighting for our fairytales, I want to hear what amazing adventures you are pursuing. Each and every one of you are going to create some amazing, beautiful fairytales. You are going to change your lives, and hopefully our world.

I hope this process helps both of us. Your active participation in this book reminds me that what I put into the world is valuable. As a writer with near constant imposter syndrome, that is SO BIG. You have no idea the blessing you will be bestowing on me.

For you, I hope you will suddenly realize that even if you have been thinking you are alone, you now have one person who is aware of your goal and desperately rooting for you to achieve it. I'm your everyday fairytale's biggest fan!!!

Nemirah smirks as you snag the parchment for the LOST COW off the board.

"What?" you ask. "I'd like to start small. Maybe on top of ten silver, they'll offer a bit of fresh milk or cheese for our trouble."

Nemirah and Jonathan nod. It sounds smart enough.

Together you wave good-bye to the barkeep and head out into the sunshine of the village. Orik already sits up front in the cart and shades his eyes to look at you. Jonathan jumps up beside him and immediately grabs the reins.

"Oh no, you're not driving."

Orik crosses his arms over his chest. "You take one wrong turn and break a wagon wheel and you're never trusted again."

"In bandit country, no less."

Orik grunts.

Nemirah helps you up into the back of the cart. "Time to get comfortable."

LEVEL TWELVE - BUILDING YOUR PARTY

Finding Your People

> *"Books! And cleverness! There are more*
> *important things – friendship and bravery."*

FROM HERMIONE GRANGER IN J.K. ROWLING'S
HARRY POTTER AND THE SORCERER'S STONE

In the sunny valley between the mountains, the path is wide and well-worn. Wagon wheels have driven deep rivets in the dirt. Luckily, the plentiful hooves of horses, mules, and donkeys have ground down any major bumps. Along either side of the road now that the town has fallen away, there are only glowing fields of young wheat and open ranges of green with the speckles of mini white clouds that are sheep.

The mountains still appear small in the distance, but you wonder if you will reach them before nightfall or if you will have to camp the first night out here in the open land. It is hard to judge how the time will pass since you are so used to traveling on foot. At this point, you are intensely grateful for the new method of transportation that you have secured for yourself.

Sitting in the back of the wagon with Nemirah, you lean back and appreciate the sunshine warming your bones. You roll up your sleeves, soaking it all in. You must have fallen asleep in a pleasant morning nap because a touch to your shoulder makes you jerk awake.

"Our turn up front," Nemirah says.

The wagon has come to a halt at the side of the road. The position of the sun tells you it's a little bit after midday. Jonathan and Orik exchange places with you and Nemirah as they pull fresh rations of bread and salted meat out of their packs for a little lunch.

"Not get enough sleep last night?" Jonathan laughs. "You turned in earlier than all of us."

You snort, but still find you are wiping the sleep out of your eyes.

"Oh, give 'em a break, Jonathan." Orik defends you. "When was the last time you went off traveling all by yourself and decided to put all your cards in with a bunch of strangers?"

Jonathan waves Orik off.

Nemirah takes the reins and you settle beside her, taking a drink from your canteen. Despite just filling it this morning, the liquid inside is already reflecting the leathery nature of its container.

"How long have you been working together?" you ask as the wagon gets moving again.

Orik speaks through bites of bread and meat, more than enough crumbs getting into his beard. You find yourself chuckling at this VERY dwarfish behavior. "Lila and I have known Serge and Marx since they were tikes. They've been in town their whole lives, the baker's lad and her wife's cousin's kid."

"Serge wasn't needed helping at the bakery?"

"Nah, Janey's got her two elder daughters keeping the place in top shape. One of the local farmers requested the boys for shepherding, but when I mentioned adventuring…well, I won."

Jonathan continues, "We give them straightforward and easy journeys for the most part for now. There is a good stretch of safe and open road between Rushbar, Flemkit, and Kahln where they can take carts of goods for trade. They're chomping at the bit for some monster hunting, but I'm not going to be the one to send some teens to their deaths."

Nemirah rolls her eyes. "Nah, you'll just try to send me to my death."

"My love! Never! Although, you are the best we got for a good reconnaissance."

Nemirah laughs. You glance between them. Is there something between them? Nemirah catches your look and waves your thought away. "I wouldn't touch Jonathan with the end of a lance."

Jonathan feigns shock and disappointment. "Believe me, there are many who are happy to take your place."

"Sure, plenty of competition."

Jonathan crosses his hands behind his head as he leans back, getting comfortable. "There is. When was the last time we went to the city together? I will tell you—"

"There will be a pining woman waiting to crawl back to you?" Nemirah asks, a smirk still touching the corner of her mouth.

"Yeah, actually."

Nemirah jerks a thumb at him while explaining to you. "We picked up the ladies' man in Dain. Probably got a little too handsy with someone he shouldn't. He was being surrounded by three brothers in an alley when I stepped in to defend him."

Orik tries to press Nemirah's buttons. "And why did you step in to defend him?"

Jonathan raises his eyebrows, another smile on his lips.

"Because three against one isn't fair odds."

"You're my hero!" Jonathan exclaims.

"And don't you forget it."

You turn fully to Nemirah. "When did you get involved in all this?"

Nemirah's eyes turn wistful, like she is watching a pleasant memory from her past play behind her eyes. "I had a bounty and when I showed up, he was there."

Orik lifts a hand and waves it. "Guilty."

"There was a bounty out *for you*?" you ask in shock.

"There was. I may have had a few…misplaced…words with an elf in my youth. And as you would expect…the pointy ear still hasn't given up the grudge."

"Still? So," you continue to Nemirah, "you didn't turn him in?"

"I made him pay the bounty—clear his name. It was stupid not to."

"The elf wanted money from you?"

"I may have stolen some leather armor," Orik grunts as he crosses his arms over his chest. Your eyes slowly rove over the fine leather pauldrons on his shoulders. Orik catches your gaze. "Yes, this leather armor."

Laughter erupts from all in the wagon.

Finding your people is like finding a solace in the storm of life. There are friends who come and go, but then there are the true party members who always stick with us. They may go different ways and travel along different paths, but when you come back together it is like no time has passed at all.

I have several wonderful friendships like this—two amazing women I have known since preschool and first grade. Our lives have separated and grown apart, but I know I could turn to them in an instant and that they would be ready to come to my side again just like when we were in grade school.

My three best friends from college are the same. Our friendship is the kind that can traverse mountains and oceans and never feel thin. It is the type of friendship that can have the hard conversations with understanding and trust, can weather the tears and the hardships of life, and still always come out on top.

I pray that you are also blessed one day with friendships like this. However, sometimes on the journey there are stretches where we are alone. One reason why you have asked a fictional character to walk alongside you, is because YOU are in control of that, and they NEVER have to leave your side.

But in the real world, there will be times in your tale when you have to purposefully build a friendship that is new in order to have some extra support while you pursue your everyday fairytale. That is what we are going to work on in this chapter.

Maybe your closest friends support your desire to go to graduate school, but they don't wish to actually attend with you. Voila! Time to find a graduate school friend who wants to take classes with you, read all your homework assignments, and exchange feedback! You know where you will find this person? Once you actually show up to school the first day!

Unlike mentors, weak ties, or brief acquaintances, with whom we might have to behave with a certain elevated air of professionalism or tact, the friendships we are looking for are the type that can be real or messy.

Building your party means finding a place to be yourself with a group of people who respect you exactly as you are.

I will admit this is not necessarily going to be easy, but again, an awareness of what you are looking for and what you need often brings this into your life faster. Remember, just like if you start thinking about red Volkswagens, you will start to SEE red Volkswagens everywhere!

So while making new friends can be scary, especially as an adult, let's get focused on exactly what sort of party members you need moving forward.

SESSION RECAP:

We're back to our journals to put together a little list because as you grow in confidence and start knocking out your everyday fairytale, you are going to start getting ideas for bigger and tougher goals. However, as you start reaching for a bigger adventure, the problem always falls down to something along the lines of…"I've never done this before! I don't know what I am doing! How am I supposed to get from point A to point B?"

The answer is very simple.

<u>You</u> might not know the way, but <u>someone else does</u>.

That's a beautiful thing, because you don't have to recreate the wheel. You can do your research and then follow in their footsteps.

For example, I attended graduate school for screenwriting because I HAD NEVER WRITTEN A SCREENPLAY BEFORE and I had no idea where to start. I turned to my professors and fellow students to guide me. Now, I understand the craft on a far deeper level than I would have just stumbling around on my own. The cool thing is, I also get to repay the favor. Several of my professors and cohort members have asked for my assistance and guidance when writing a novel (more of my wheelhouse and expertise), because that is something THEY have never done before.

Now, unlike when we considered direct mentors or experts, this time you are going to look for people who are truly just one step ahead of you. Who can help you with your first next step and then ALSO walk alongside you as you journey together?

For example, in *A Court of Silver Flames*, Nesta had only just begun her warrior fitness training program when she invited other interested women along to join her. She was only one step ahead, but together the women grew to something incredible.

Building the right party may take time, especially if it is going to come down to building some relationships with people you don't know yet. So be patient and take your time. Do this right. For now, we are just going to research, collect, and make a list.

For your current everyday fairytale…

Who do you know that is already doing what you want to be doing?

They might be direct contacts—family members, friends, coworkers, acquaintances. Or they might be complete strangers—another person at the gym you've never talked to, a leader of a training program, or people you follow on social media.

Write as many names as you can think of. You can refer back to this list later and find exactly the right moment (or the right concern) to reach out.

When you are ready, start by picking one person on your list and asking them a single question. For example, what would they do in this unique situation? Or where would they turn to get started?

Don't expect more. Don't expect them to immediately take you under their wing.

Just ask for the favor.

Ask for their advice on something small.

Then, leave it be for a while. If it's someone on social media, keep loving on their content and interacting, but don't send direct messages every day.

Over time, your relationship will develop and you can ask another question and another.

You will be amazed when you suddenly have a whole posse of people looking to walk alongside you. It feels crazy—like it came out of the blue. I will admit that wholeheartedly when two professors that I look up to like no other asked for my assistance on a writing project. WHAT? Little old me? Your student??? It is a long slog of trusting in the daily work you put in, and then suddenly opportunity arises.

SIDE QUEST:

You're in luck though! You have this book in your hands! While you are slowly building your party out there in the wide scary world, you have a community right here that is already primed and excited to walk by your side. Who knows, you may even be surprised to meet the key players who will be helping you make big strides in your journey in the coming days!

So, head to our resource page where I will be including all the materials mentioned in this book as well as others I find along the way at colleenochab.com/fairytaleresources. Then, start by joining our Discord server, the "Fight for the Fairytale Community," make a post to introduce yourself, and invite someone else to walk with you! It is likely that there will be MANY who are also trying to tackle a similar goal / everyday fairytale as you and would be willing to offer their support and advice.

Depending on when you are getting your hands on this book, our Discord community may be small or already growing. For those who are coming in as our starting members with the original release of this book, thank you for participating when our group is still small. I am so grateful for the work you put in to make this community the lovely place it will become. You are my party members, my fellow warriors, and I am proud to walk alongside you because I have felt your support from the beginning.

"So let me get this straight," you continue a few hours later. Nemirah has since given you control of the reins, and you're pretty proud of your ability to guide the cart horse. Even if the road so far has only been straight and easy. "Lila had the shop, and she offered Orik a job collecting rare herbs and other materials for her, not knowing about the bounty."

"Where I fell in love with her and asked her to marry me," Orik includes.

"But not before I almost turned him in for the bounty on his head," Nemirah says. "And a few years later, while Orik and I were working on bounties together—"

Jonathan quirks a thumb at himself. "Nem saved my skin from some brutish characters."

"And lastly you hired Serge and Marx."

Orik smiles. "You got it."

"Seems like a group of ragtag weirdos that you've shaped into a well-oiled machine."

"Took years to do it, but sure." Your stomach growls as the sun starts to dip below the horizon. Orik taps your shoulder. "And look at this wonderful new cog I've found to fit right in."

You cannot help the swell of pride that fills your chest as you smile back at him. "It would seem so."

"Now come on, let's camp down that ridge line over there. Those rocks should protect us from the wind during the night."

Craft Your Tracking System

*"Experience is the only thing that brings
knowledge, and the longer you are on earth
the more experience you are sure to get..."*

FROM THE WIZARD IN L. FRANK BAUM'S
THE WONDERFUL WIZARD OF OZ

The conversation and laughter around the campfire that night is easy, comfortable, and engaging. You have all settled and laid out your bedrolls in a circle around the small pit of stones that Orik has put together. Jonathan has tended the horse. A warm, little fire now crackles between you.

Behind the natural ridge, the wind is indeed blocked, and the natural landmark shelters you, but you can still hear it whistling above. In the sky, there is just darkness and stars. No clouds. No threat of rain. The land here at your campsite was leveled and trampled, so no doubt this is a common stopping point for travelers along the road.

You pull out your map and try to make note of it, even though your map is way too large and lacking in details to really be useful.

It's as the stories naturally flow that you begin to realize just how accomplished and experienced your companions truly are. It was luck that you stumbled upon them. Right place and right time and all that. Because in any other situation, you would be sure that no one with this level of expertise would invite you, the naive beginner adventurer, along for the journey.

Orik has nearly forty years of adventuring under his belt. His scars tell many of the stories. Time as a sailor and a fight with a kraken. A crazy adventure on the back of a scaly dragon. A hunt for a hydra through a deadly cave system. You doubt he could run out of stories to tell you. Though you are sure he is embellishing some of them, you don't catch the twinge of an outright lie anywhere throughout his storytelling.

Jonathan, though his stories do often revolve around taverns and beautiful, alluring partners, is well-read and has clearly attended some college in a big city on one of the continents. He speaks with an air of educated authority, but not in a way that might be overbearing or superior. You know the troop likely relies upon him for facts and details about particular animals or monsters, as well as plants, herbs, and other materials.

Nemirah is a quiet, elusive mystery. She doesn't share much and seems to have a skillful ease of turning the conversation back to other people without outright making it appear like she's doing it. If you had to guess, especially with her knife throwing skills, you would say that she was a trained assassin in some underground society or guild, but you definitely aren't bold enough to ask.

For a moment, the difference in your abilities and skillsets makes you pause. What right do you have to sit here among these warriors? Then you remember young Serge and Marx, whom you know the group still carefully manages to protect them from unnecessary harm. The 'twins' are at a stage in their life where they can do more protected exploring. For you, though, the time is now to take some risks and try something new. That's it, you remind yourself. That's why you are here traveling with Orik, Jonathan, and Nemirah and not transporting goods with Serge and Marx.

This group believes you are capable enough to assist them. You are going to prove that they didn't put their trust in the wrong person.

Life is not a game, and certainly most days I wouldn't claim it was necessarily fun. We know life is serious and choices have consequences, but what if you could do your best to make even the difficult days have a softened edge? What if the negative connotation of consequences could be reconfigured as experience? What would that do to lighten your load?

That is precisely why I love the quote from *The Wonderful Wizard of Oz*, "The more life we live, the more experience we get." If you think of it like the wonderful old crone in a fantasy book that says, "Listen here, young ones, while I tell you a story…" it would be pretty darn cool to reach that stage of life and look back and appreciate all that experience you have accumulated.

This train of thinking also makes me remember comedian Eliza Shlesinger, who has a bit about being an "elder millennial." She says, "Elder millennial. Wizened. Sage. Yes, gather round the Snapchat children. I'll tell you the tale of the landline!"

Sure, it's a joke, but it's true. The more life you have lived, the more you have experienced. In the end, you have the CHOICE to let your experiences make you closed off, angry, and hardened OR worldly, empathetic, and encouraging. We have seen this in SO many stories. There are the characters who face tragedy or hardship and turn off or turn away. Then, there are those who rise, defy odds, and keep living. Often, that tends to be the difference between the hero and the villain.

I would like to show you how to track some of your experiences, at least in a small way, to help you see what progress you are actually making along the journey. Because remember, when we are in the dark forest, it is easy to get so blinded by the trees that we forget how much distance we have actually covered.

❧━━❧

SIDE QUEST & SESSION RECAP:

For this chapter, our side quest and session recap are tied into one because as you figure out which tracker system is right for you, you're going to be doing A LOT of reflecting—not only on yourself but on the goal you are trying to achieve at the moment.

Hear me out, as I would categorize myself as hyper-organized, plans too much, Type A personality. By no means am I saying that more people should behave like me…because to be honest, life is meant to be lived, not planned for in a spreadsheet. I know where my faults lie! That's why Leona is still in my corner helping me fight for my fairytale, because I could definitely benefit from learning how to chill and just enjoy the moment. Not to say Leona is any better at it than me! That's why we are party members. We are figuring it all out together.

If the word spreadsheet just made you go "ICK!" don't worry! I have a number of different options that you can take advantage of to suit your mood or your personality. And actually, in this chapter, no spreadsheet! Though for D&D peeps, you might actually like the spreadsheet idea—don't worry, that's coming up in Level Nineteen when you are ready to face your big goal! *Wink Wink!*

A tracking system of some kind is an ideal way to start taking the baby steps toward your goal. Especially for a little everyday fairytale adventure like we are starting out with, this tracker will be relatively uncomplicated and straightforward. Though I guess, of course, it depends on what type of tracker you choose to make! The control is in your hands.

Here are two simple options to get you started. Try one of these for now, and like I said, I am going to introduce you to a *slightly* bigger system later so you truly get the RPG vibe I promised in this book.

Option A: Wall calendar or simple habit tracker

Let's say for this example that your goal is to walk 5,000 steps a day each and every day for the next three months. A simple wall calendar or habit tracker might be just the thing for you since you will be able to put a nice, pretty X over the day each time you hit your goal. This type of tracking would also be useful for other goals like: "I ate three meals today," "I made my bed today," "I took a shower and took care of myself today," etc. Don't let anyone, not even me, pressure you on the nature of your everyday fairytale. You are fighting for YOUR fairytale.

The visual nature of this type of tracker is great because (I don't know about you but...) I would hate to see the blank space. So this type of system would put a nice, subtle pressure on me to get things done even when I don't feel like doing it.

If you would like a printable habit tracker, I have included a template I designed on my website that you can download for free. It even has a space to glue a picture of the character that is walking alongside you as well as a quote from them to keep you motivated.

You can hang this habit tracker OR your wall calendar on the fridge or anywhere else you will see it regularly and refer to it.

But here's the catch! If you are going the wall calendar route, make sure there is space in the margins of your calendar. In the next chapter, we are going to be discussing crafting a reward system for yourself. We are going to need some extra space! The reward system is already built into my printable download, so you don't have to worry if you are going that route.

Option B: Your wall covered with sticky notes

This is a personal favorite of mine because as a writer, I like to plot out entire books and series on the wall in my office. I am sure my partner just 'adores' the clutter (with an eye roll attached), but to me the variety of colors make the story exciting. The visual nature of the wall reminds me where the story was and, of course, where it is headed next. Also, it doesn't feel as restricting as a formal outline because I can move the sticky notes around at any time! We love a bit of impermanence!

This tracker is ideal for people who are working toward everyday fairytales that don't have a set, repetitive task to do every day. For example, if you have a small goal to research and apply for a grant, this could take the form of one: a sticky note about collecting resources, two: a sticky note about reading certain help articles, three: a sticky note about compiling your documents, four: a sticky note for printing those documents, and so on, and so on. Since each of these tasks are different, the wall calendar or habit tracker route probably won't be very helpful. And, you can always move the sticky notes around, swap them out, or add to them!

Need a smaller version because your partner, roommate, or parents don't want sticky notes on their walls??? Buy mini sticky notes and a little poster board from an office supply store!

So how would this example work for achieving your goal? Here's my recommendations, but you can adjust this to suit your style as well as your needs.

1. Mark a few sticky notes in one color (I chose teal) to stand as the markers of your timeline. For example, if you want to achieve your goal in three months, you might put three sticky notes to mark the end of month one, month two, and month three. Or maybe you want to break it down even more? So put up twelve sticky notes, one for each week! These sticky notes are going to act as your check-in moments. (Gosh Colleen, how many times can you say sticky notes in one chapter?!)

2. Pick a different sticky note color for each type of activity! For my example above, I might use yellow for research, green for at home/office work, and purple for scheduled meetings or activities done outside of the home. Place the sticky notes along the timeline where appropriate. So research might populate month one, while month two and three would have more green and purple!

There they are, your two options! Pick one of these for now or adapt one of them to suit your needs. Just like with the rest of this book, as we move forward we will see things change and adapt, so don't feel bad about starting off with one method and switching to another. That's precisely why I am introducing my "spreadsheet" system later.

"So," Nemirah begins, turning her questioning eyes on you, "what about you? Where are you from? What's your story? How did you end up...here?"

You stare at the fire for a long moment before answering.

"A coastal town, a ways south of Dain."

"So you're a fair sailor."

"I wouldn't say that. I get queasy the moment the waves grow too choppy."

Jonathan raises a hand. "Same here. Same here."

"So..." Nemirah presses.

"I studied under a tutor, a healer for a while. Morgana Elswere."

"No way!" Jonathan exclaims. "THE Morgana Elswere?"

You laugh but nod. "Yes, though to me she's just Auntie Mor." The others' eyes widen. "I was a good pupil, but I just got antsy cooped up in the cabin all day waiting and never knowing what was going to walk in the door next."

"Do you know how amazing that is?" Jonathan asks. "She's famous."

You can't argue with him. It is pretty amazing, you suddenly realize. Morgana taught you everything you know about herbs and healing, and knife work actually. She saw how you were staring outside at the open country secretly, and maybe not so secretly, wanting more.

She had suggested you go out and see the world.

Now you are even more grateful for her than you were before, because you truly do have a knowledge, and not only that, but an interesting past, just like all the others.

The Reward of Success,
Even a Small One

*"You're golden, sweetheart. You're going to
have sponsors lined up around the block."*

FROM HAYMITCH ABERNATHY IN SUZANNE
COLLINS' THE HUNGER GAMES

You step out of the darkness of a cave a few days later and blink into the sunshine. Orik grins from ear to ear as he carries the head of a cave troll that nearly doesn't fit in his finely muscled arms. Like one of the strong men at a fair, he carries it like one would an atlas stone carry. His face is filled with pride.

Nemirah carefully tucks the vials of troll saliva that she collected into her bag.

"Look at that," Jonathan says. "Two birds, one stone. Saliva for Lila and a dead troll for Orik."

"I told you that's why I took the bounty!" Orik argues as he heaves the head into the back of the cart. "A troll fight and keeping my lady happy, nothing better!"

"You're such a romantic, Orik." Nemirah laughs, but then she sees how close the cave troll head is to the bench where you will have to sit for at least the next few hours. "You're kidding. Can't it sit up front with the two of you?"

Jonathan climbs into the front and lifts the reins. "There is absolutely no room on this bench—especially with Orik's girth."

"Are you saying I'm getting fat?"

"Comfortable," Jonathan argues. "The pounds have been coming since having a beautiful lady home-cooking you meals."

"I would say I'm plenty agile!" Orik settles into the front of the cart with Jonathan. "Did you see the leaping hit I did to finish that old bugger!"

Nemirah shoves the cave troll head with a foot to give you room to sidle onto the bench in the back of the cart beside her.

"We're only a few hours outside of Treg. The bounty is due there," Jonathan explains. "The stink shouldn't get too bad."

Nemirah feigns covering her mouth and nose. "Cave trolls are bad enough alive."

You laugh alongside the crew as you set off to collect the bounty.

When you reach the outskirts of Treg, the rich estate owner pays Orik handsomely for the head of the cave troll. Though it appears, besides to prove that your crew actually killed the troll, that the estate owner wants nothing to do with the head. He forces Orik to carry it around to the back of the barn, where a stable hand lifts an eyebrow and frowns when you tell him the master of the estate has said he would burn it. The young man recovers quickly and directs Orik to drop the head into a pit as he starts collecting wood for a fire.

As a reward for your assistance, Orik pockets most of the coin, but pays for dinner for the whole crew at one of the nicest taverns in town that night as well as rooms. It's as you settle in your comfortable bed after having a belly filled with warm, delicious food as well as a bath to wash off the road, that you are suddenly incredibly pleased about the fight with the cave troll.

If someone would have asked any earlier, you might have said the fighting, the odor, and the uncomfortable trip in the back of the wagon wasn't worth the bounty. Now that you are reaping the rewards, though, the thought doesn't even cross your mind.

You can see how Orik, Nemirah, and Jonathan got tangled up in this life. It's challenging and difficult some of the time, but it certainly has its rewards, which must be what makes it so darn addicting.

Do you remember reading *The Hunger Games* or watching the movie and experiencing the moment where the parachute falls, revealing a gift for the tribute? These sponsor gifts—with anything from food to medicine to weapons—were delivered by silver parachutes into the arena as a way to engage the citizens to interact with the Games. However, to the tribute, they were rewards for surviving, for surpassing a major trial. Rewards generate hope and a sense of happiness. While President Snow used it as a means to manipulate the tributes, we can use the tactic in a much "kinder" yet still mentally manipulative way!

We can set rewards for ourselves to help us fight through difficult patches to reach milestones in our goals. If some of the action steps toward your goals are NOT exactly things you would willingly choose to do on a normal day, you have to come up with a reason to go through the "hardship."

Living in my crazy, type A mind, I often fail to celebrate the little wins along the way. I've done this with school, with extracurricular activities, and with hobbies. I treat the goal as the ultimate destination, and fail to appreciate the beautiful countryside of the journey as I travel along to reach it.

Have you ever found yourself thinking this way? It's not the best way to live.

I struggled hard with this topic during my cancer journey, because of course I just wanted to be at the end! I wanted to be cancer-free! The truth, though, was I was still living every minute of each and every day. The end wasn't coming any faster. And, there were wonderful moments with friends and family that I would have missed constantly thinking about that seemingly magical end date.

So instead, focusing on tiny mile markers was the way to go. For example, shortly after I lost my hair, my partner and I were to attend a wedding. My best friend spent the afternoon with me to go shopping for a wig that made me feel beautiful. We went to the wedding even though I was tired from a recent treatment. It ended up being great to get out of the house, and though we turned in early, I am glad I didn't miss it. These moments are the ones we'll cherish.

We need to check in often, reflect on our progress, and celebrate the little wins. Heck, we even need to celebrate the failures. As a writer whose career is just starting, I have started tracking every "no" I receive, because every "no" is one step closer to "yes."

As we track, we also need to reward.

Just like in a fantasy adventure where the hero receives a reward for completing the bounty, so, too, are you going to reward yourself for hitting certain milestones toward your goal. That's why we divided up the tracker the way we did. So now, let's refer back to it!

SESSION RECAP:

This is a check-in! I'm waving my little checkpoint flag. Come hang out and save your game!

If you have been reading this book in one go without implementing the activities, you won't be ready for this yet, but I see you. Entirely valid. We each have to approach this process in the way that works best for us. If you are going the READ THE ENTIRE THING FIRST route, I encourage you to re-read at a slower pace, moving chapter by chapter, and actually complete the session recaps and side quests as you go on your second pass.

For those of you who have been moving slowly, chapter by chapter, already, this is your time to sit back and evaluate perhaps the first few days of your everyday fairytale, or maybe the first week or so.

Have you been doing the activities you said you were going to be doing? If yes, we're going to celebrate and keep up the great work.

If not, what's going wrong? What's standing in your way? What do we need to adjust moving forward to make the hard work happen?

There is literally NO GUILT here, because on the journey, we are going to be CONSTANTLY adapting. So if your first plan doesn't work out for you, you didn't fail, you succeeded! You are figuring out what is not working, and every step is the right step along the journey. Sometimes we have to move sideways or even backward to propel ourselves ahead later.

SIDE QUEST:

Create your reward system! Yahoo! This step is fun!

Let's return to the tracking method that you chose in the last chapter. Whether you are using a calendar, a habit tracker, or a wall of sticky notes—it's time to add to it!

While there is no right way to do this, I am going to share with you a few basic examples. Tweak and adapt to suit your style! You also know yourself. Would more rewards help you achieve your goals? Add a bunch! Want to spread things out so you really cherish when you hit a reward? Do it that way!

Rewards are like completing your bounties. You do a task; you earn a reward. The scope and size of the reward varies by the task achieved.

If you are using the calendar, move ahead seven days from the date you started and add a note—REWARD #1! This is your first checkpoint. If you reach it here, completing your tasks, you have earned a reward. You can work the same way with the habit tracker. Mark when you have completed seven habits in a row. If you are going the sticky note route, you may want to add the reward to the bottom of each sticky note.

It is entirely up to you how you wish to set up when you receive your rewards.

The rewards that you choose are also going to be unique to you. I will include here a short list of rewards that I might include for myself, but depending on your personality, hobbies, life-situation, etc., this is going to look very different for everyone. Your rewards also don't have to cost any money, so try to take budgeting into consideration here.

My examples:

- Take a bath with a special bath bomb

- Go out for an ice cream cone to share with my partner

- An evening off from writing to read a book I have been craving to start

- Buy myself flowers, a new water bottle, or a book

- Mindlessly scroll TikTok for an hour with no guilt

For your rewards, do your best to include things that are not in your normal routine. Reward yourself with things that might feel too luxurious, or something you wouldn't normally do. For example, in my list, I NEVER take a bath—always a shower—so spending time just soaking in the tub without having to be anywhere else seems like a luxury to me.

What kinds of rewards are going to help you hit the checkpoints of your everyday fairytale? Make 'em good and make 'em you.

The next day you leave Treg to travel the forested mountain pass toward Kahln. It is a long, slow day since your crew decides to not push the little cart horse too hard pulling your weight up the mountain. The horse is a tough, shaggy thing, and going at the slower pace, he doesn't fatigue. The crew decides to continue on a little into the night after sunset, since the openings in the trees allow enough starlight to reach the ground to guide the way.

You are keeping your eyes peeled because these are the woods where the cow on your own bounty was said to have disappeared, or at least run off to. However, as the clouds start to roll in above, you give up hope of seeing it for the evening. As the path starts to descend down the other side of the mountain, you finally rein the horse in.

No use accidentally rolling off a cliff now that the starlight has all but disappeared. You start to wonder if you are in for rain or some sort of coming storm.

Everyone begins to empty out the cart and prepare the space around to make camp. As your crew sets to their work and their own jobs, a quiet, comfortable silence falls over the trees.

LEVEL FIFTEEN - STAKING
YOUR VAMPIRES

Sometimes the Suckers
Need to Get Dealt With

"Evil has only the power that we give it."

FROM WILL HALLOWAY IN RAY BRADBURY'S
SOMETHING WICKED THIS WAY COMES

Then, there is a rushing in the woods around you. At first everyone
remains quiet. It is so dark, it is hard to see anything besides the shapes
and silhouettes of your companions beside you. But something is not
right, especially not as one in your company screams. You can hear
Orik fumbling with his flint and steel, swearing, trying desperately
to light his torch. The rushing is accompanied by screeching—fast,
sharp sounds that echo through the woods.

You almost don't lift your knife in time to the figure that rushes
toward your face. Then, the steel catches on two sharp fangs. They
clamp down with a sickening clang. In the dim light, two eyes flash
before you—far, far too close. They are red. Vampires.

You shout it aloud to the group and you hear a collective groan. Yes, this was unexpected. This was not at all the quarry you were hunting for. You are all definitely ill-prepared to fight vampires. They're undead, right? How do you kill something that is already dead?

You shove the creature back and swing. It deftly moves out of the way and lunges for you again. It's spindly and fast, yet somehow moves like a cockroach. The odd image makes you want to vomit, but you don't have time because its claws swipe your arm. Pain rockets through your skin.

You duck as the teeth flash for your neck again. You slash your knife forward and cut across a hard belly. A cold liquid spills across your fingers as a horrific hiss reaches your ears.

Then suddenly, the forest is lit with the brightest of light. You blink toward it, trying to make out the source, as the vampire before you shies away, nearly collapsing to the ground and crawling away to the shadows. Your eyes are drawn to its sickening, pale flesh.

There is more hissing in the woods all around you. Yes, many more vampires. You can see the shadowy figures between all the trees now. Some of them turn to run from the light, but others clearly are angered by it. Perhaps ten or more quickly rush for it.

You see the light bob. From your perspective, it looks like the morning sun is bobbing and weaving through the forest. You have to avert your gaze to not be blinded.

You are shocked by a sudden hiss on your right as another set of fangs goes for your arm. You bring up your knife, but it is too late.

With a ring in the air at the last moment, another dagger sails out of the darkness and strikes the vampire in the neck just in time to distract it from its attack on you. The vampire screeches as it pulls the dagger out. There is a foaming coming from the wound. The creature scratches at its neck.

You blink and the dagger disappears. It was there one moment, and then suddenly it was gone.

A thin, gangly elf appears beside you. His reddish-brown hair glows close to orange in the daylight alighting the forest. He hands you a wooden stake already coated in the same dark liquid that had spilled across your hand and presses you back as five more of the creatures burst out the woods toward you, avoiding the light.

"Stab 'em with that. Get it in the heart—you win," he says breathlessly. With a dash, he is flinging himself into the group of approaching vampires again with a near reckless abandon.

You cannot help but watch him. He deftly swings his daggers, cutting close and throwing far. Each time he throws, the weapon appears back on his belt where he pulls it again. It's like a dance. Except a deadly one. Even facing off against vampires, he is keeping an eye on the daylight a ways away.

As you shake yourself out of the shock and lift the wooden stake in your dominant hand, you set to work helping him finish off these creatures of the night. There are just a few of them left when the daylight is suddenly snuffed and you are plunged into pitch blackness again.

"Leona!" You hear the elf shout through the woods.

You try to keep fighting, but your strikes are missing. Your eyes were so adjusted to that bright daylight that now you can't even see shadows.

The last few vampiric survivors are growing bold now that the light has disappeared. You feel a strike to your torso. Your mind is playing tricks on you. You are picturing them as fangs when it clearly was a set of five claws. Blindly, you plunge the wooden stake toward the creature. It cries out—a mangled sort of moan—and clinging to it, you wrestle it to the ground. You lift and stab again, quite possibly the most violent thing you have ever done. It is unlike you, but death is on the line.

Suddenly the creature goes still below you. It ceases to draw breath. Breathless yourself, you gather to your feet. There is a growing silence. You listen carefully for more hissing and rustling, but none reaches your ears.

There is another strike and snap. It makes you jump, but this time Orik does successfully light his torch on fire. It illuminates a small circle. You immediately assess your companions. You all stand. There are vampires lying still on the ground all around you.

The thin, russet-haired elf pulls a wooden stake out of one vampire at his feet. He stands and considers you all. "Nice work," he pants. Then directly to you he says, "You are quick on your feet."

You nod to him in thanks. "I could say the same about you."

Through the darkness, a woman seems to materialize out of thin air. She is also an elf with tall, pointed ears and intensely sharp features, standing six feet tall. Her silver white hair is streaked with blood. Her face is hard, her eyes wild as she picks through your small circle, assessing. "We must work quickly," she says as she spots you.

You flinch back as she rushes to your side, so fast she's like a wraith in the night. The elven woman pauses apologetically. "I'm sorry." She slows her movements and lifts her hands to show she holds no weapon against you. "You were struck. Any bites?"

You look down and assess your injuries for the first time. There are several places where the claws got you, but thankfully no bites. You tell her the same.

She nods, and her hands work quickly, offering you herbs and salve and clean cloth to bandage your wounds before she turns to the others.

Eventually, everyone confirms they have made it through intact without a bite, and the woman relaxes a little. As you tend to yourself, you watch her gather the vampires one body at a time, stacking them together in the woods. Some of the others in your party help her.

Then at long last, when Orik touches the torch to the stack of bodies and the small bonfire illuminates the trees, the elven woman finally settles, sitting at the base of a tree and leaning her head back. Her breathing is still heavy. You watch the elven man approach her side. He checks her for injuries, though she tries to wave him away. He crouches at her side and uses a canteen to wash blood pooling from a scrape on her arm.

"You're the hunter," Orik says as he settles on a log. "The one that came through town. The Night Wolf."

The woman looks up at him with serious eyes. "Yes," she says with a voice like waves hitting rocks at the seashore. It is both gravelly and jarring, as well as honed and soothing. "I am Mereoleona Valerien. Last surviving child of Mirazeiros Valerien and eldest daughter of Omatoris Luria of Eschol. But now they just call me the Night Wolf." The man settles beside her against the tree as she gestures to him. "This is Raololen Montenn. Eldest son of the house of Montenn and its last surviving heir."

Jonathan whispers under his breath. "Don't need to know your whole life story."

Her head whips toward him. "It is customary among my people to introduce yourself by lineage of your ancestors, especially those who have passed on. But yes, you don't need to know that."

Jonathan dips his head to her, slightly chastised. "What shall we call you then?"

"Leona and Rao are just fine," Rao says carefully.

"How long have you both been hunting vampires?"

The two glance at each other. "Too long," they say in unison.

Leona laughs as she stretches her legs out toward their makeshift, morbid bonfire. "But someone's got to do the world's dirty work."

Well, here we are. You have finally met my dear Leona. She can tell you, dealing with vampires sucks. Literally. But you have to fight them, or the suckers will get you instead.

I wrote Leona's backstory for our campaign well before I was diagnosed with cancer. I decided she was going to be a druid warrior, and as I read more about druids, it said some of their primary enemies were creatures of the night like vampires and even beholders (a monster that appears as a floating orb with a large mouth, a single central eye, and many smaller eyestalks on top). So, my mind created Leona's personal hatred for vampires by crafting a story where a traveling group of them killed her family, leaving her to set out on her own—and thus step into the campaign of my Game Master.

Once I was diagnosed with breast cancer, I was starting to notice an eerie correlation. Just as vampires suck blood and drain one's literal life force, so, too, was chemotherapy draining my energy from me. Though my port saved my life (I absolutely hate needles and always feel like I am going to pass out when doctors have to draw blood), every time I went into the oncologist's office, the nurses had to access the port, stab me with a needle, and pump life-saving medication into my body that also happened to make me feel sick and tired. Allergic to one of my medications, I was hopped up on Benadryl and weary for the hours that I sat there in that chair. In the days that followed, I fought against all of the side effects. My blood pressure so low and getting so dehydrated that I had to go in and get stabbed in the port again for more fluids every other day. It was a miserable cycle.

Though cancer medication can be lifesaving, it is also utterly life sucking because it changes EVERYTHING about you and how you operate in daily life.

Maybe Leona was placed into my imagination by a higher power exactly for this.

I reminded myself that if Leona could continue to fight back against the blood-sucking, life-draining vampires in her life, so, too, could I fight against the effects of chemotherapy, my personal vampire.

Some vampires in our lives can only be managed. For example, my chemo was a literal physical vampire, and one that I couldn't necessarily get rid of. The same goes for other diseases, some pre-existing conditions, physical limitations, and a number of other roadblocks in life.

In this chapter, though, I want you to think about the vampires that you *could* cut out of your life, or at least control a little bit. These are the ones we have the power to tackle on this part of your journey.

What are the things (or people) in your life that drain your energy? What things are distracting you from your everyday fairytale or holding you back?

Is it getting wrapped up in endlessly scrolling on social media? Is it complaining about your job to your friends or whoever will listen? Is it watching the news first thing when you get up or right before you go to bed?

Maybe it's something a little bit deeper, and a little bit more complicated and hard to get rid of...anxiety, depression, and other mental illnesses that you can't just tell to go away and *poof*. No, they are going to take some real effort to struggle against.

These are the vampires of our lives.

We each have our own unique set, specific to us. Because what may seem like a minor roadblock to one person could be absolutely devastating and journey altering to another. That is why, just like there is no comparing your goals to another...there is also no comparing your vampires.

SESSION RECAP:

There is a theory that if you say your fears out loud that it makes them not as scary. So, let's try it for our vampires. Let's name our vampires. Call those suckers out. Hopefully, over time, their power over us will begin to lessen.

You've done a lot of soul searching up until this point, so my hope is that this will be easier than it might have been when you first picked up this book.

What in your life is draining your energy?

For me, my number one day-to-day energy sucker is negativity. When I give in to negativity, then every part of my day feels harder. I notice the bad drivers on my commute to work, every single stoplight I get stuck at, and don't get me started about arriving at the railroad tracks just to get stopped by a miles-long freight train.

You know your own vampires. Name them.

SIDE QUEST:

Now that you are mentally aware, it is time to deal the blood suckers a little blow. They are not going to hold the same power over you anymore because you are going to take ONE pointed action to pay them less mind. Without attention, you will find the vampire fights and struggles, but eventually its grip on you will lessen.

So, what is one thing that you can do to separate yourself from your vampire and give yourself some space today?

If you are not able to separate yourself, how can you be more cognizant when your vampire is around to lessen its effect on you?

When the bonfire finally burns low, everyone has had their injuries tended, and you all start to gather yourselves to move on, Rao comes over to lean beside you. "Despite not knowing anything about vampires, you sure stepped up and fought well."

"Thank you."

"We could use someone like that traveling with us. There is a lot more of that where we are going."

You glance back at your party. Suddenly, you realize you have no desire to leave them. What was once a means of moving north, these people have become your companions. You would fight for them until the bitter end. You can tell Rao and Leona feel the same way about each other.

"I appreciate the offer," you say. "But I rather like where I am at."

Rao smiles. "If you ever see any vampire bounties, feel free to take 'em. We will probably see you again."

"You both really specialize in hunting vampires? That's all you do?"

Rao considers carefully. "It's not the only thing we do, but we have a sort of personal vendetta against them. That's a story for another time."

"Well, hopefully we will meet again so I can hear it." You gesture to the smelly bonfire. "Maybe under better conditions and a tankard of ale."

"Sounds like a fair deal."

You watch Rao and Leona gather themselves and depart into the night. It is only now that their backs are turned that you notice the midnight cloak with the head of a wolf that Leona wears. The Night Wolf, indeed.

Death: Life's Greatest Teacher

*"Death is unavoidable…and it's all the
more reason for life to be lived."*

FROM VAX'ILDAN VESSAR IN CRITICAL
ROLE'S ANIMATED TV SERIES THE
LEGEND OF VOX MACHINA

It is in that moment, in the darkness, that you glimpse another outline. It's a four-legged creature with a black and white pattern across its entire body. THE COW!

You nearly leap for joy as you shout it aloud and rush off into the woods, leaving the others behind at your low burning, nasty vampire bonfire.

"Hey! Wait up!" Nemirah shouts after you, but her voice falls away in the background as you sprint between the trees.

Dang. This cow moves fast.

Your breathing huffs and your heart pumps as you finally glimpse it again. Yep, definitely a bushy tail and a lumbering gait that screams COW!

You whoop for joy! You can hear all the others following you. You found the cow! You are going to be the first one in the group to manage their personal bounty. Look at you! You know they are going to call it beginner's luck, but you don't really care.

Hiss! Screech!

You don't have time to react as the wounded vampire bursts from the trees, clawing at you viciously. You feel those claws rake over the area on your stomach that Leona had previously patched up. The skin splits open, but you feel the sharp claws curl deeper, gripping organs. You nearly vomit at the thought. It's only due to your training as a healer that you don't immediately pass out.

Another set of claws swipe across your neck and you feel the hot liquid of your own blood rush out and coat your shirt front.

You fall.

The horrible creature stands above you as it yanks its claws out. The sharp fangs flash as it smiles.

You hear Rao and Leona yelling at the others to stand back so they can handle the creature, but they sound very, very far away.

You hear your own heartbeat in your ears, but softly it fades, giving way to a static-like buzz in your ears. A warm cloak settles around your shoulders, which is comforting because in the night in the woods your extremities had been struggling against the cold. There is a growing sunlight far in the distance—and it appears a lot like the vampire hunter's daylight spell—so you rush toward it.

Sometimes life throws at us every suffering, and even though we still draw breath, it feels like we are dying inside. This feeling hits every human, no matter your race, economic status, education, or sexuality. In a way, it is something that can connect us: our suffering.

The worst possible suffering is living like you are dead when you still have the chance at life, because you never know when that time is going to be cut short.

As you know already, 2022 and 2023 were two hard years back-to-back.

I struggled my way through fertility treatment to collect my eggs just in case I find it difficult to have children later. I am glad I went through the process, but as someone who faints from needles—yeah, it sucked.

Then, on to chemotherapy, you already know about that vampire. Lost hair, low blood pressure, dehydration, and a near daily feeling of lying on the floor and never lifting my head again.

Next was a double mastectomy, where I had to wear gross tubes draining fluids from the surgery site and then stare at a body that was nothing like my own.

Following surgery number one was radiation, a daily appointment of sitting half-naked on a freezing cold table while they put a freezing, jelly-like sheet over my chest and a machine circled and whirled around me.

Throughout that time, my plastic surgeon slowly filled my breast expanders with fluid, until they were rock-hard lumps on my chest. I could literally knock someone out with them. After that, my car crash where the seat belt came down right over my port. Thank goodness everything was fine, but it still meant an out-of-pocket payment for the ambulance ride since neither me nor the driver at fault paid for additional medical car coverage. Who knew that was something you had to add on in addition to your policy?

With Leona's help, I kept my head up. Even on the days I wanted to throw in the towel and say no more, I chugged along.

It was finally my turn to do something for myself. So in a big red circle on my calendar in December 2023 was my breast reconstruction surgery. I had strategically planned it so I could have my surgery during winter break from grad school and be healed in time to head back to class in January. So, in I headed without regrets the day after my twenty-eighth birthday to have my expanders removed and my new breasts put in. This was finally something for me…to feel like myself again.

This should have been the win of the year, but life doesn't go easily. We don't know why we are chosen to suffer. I thought, for sure, 2023 was done serving me pain. I was wrong.

My mother and my fiancé did not tell me the news initially because they didn't want me to stress the day of my surgery. I understand why they did it, but throughout the day I was filled with anger. My mother wasn't coming to my surgery. Why? She's always there with me! My fiancé drove me, but he had to leave to go back to work. Why was no one here for me?

Attached to the IV and without my personal belongings, all I could do was stare out toward the nurses' station and listen in on their conversations. I know I started crying because I felt abandoned. I also was scared about going under. I bemoaned being left alone. I turned to Leona again and tried to be strong. However, throughout the day, I just got angrier.

When my fiancé came to pick me up from the recovery room and we got in the car, he finally told me the unfortunate news. The day before, on my birthday, my father had a medical emergency from a long-term disease he was managing and fell down a flight of stairs in our family basement. My fiancé let me know my father was in the ICU, but it wasn't looking good. Four days later, with me out of my own rest bed still wrapped up and trying to heal from my own surgery, we said good-bye to him in the hospital.

I was in every type of pain—physical, mental, emotional. However, I also felt numb. It wasn't cold or a lack of feeling, but rather that the world was moving by like nothing had happened, and I was just moving along with it. All I could do was pray for 2024 to be boring and for nothing eventful to happen—because I had felt enough for several decades in the span of a few months.

Death is the only guarantee in our human lives. For some, it thankfully doesn't show its face for a long, long time. I think of my friends who still have grandparents and great grandparents as they have their own kids and turn thirty or even forty.

Then there are those of us who have walked alongside Death for a long, long time—to the point where we have started to consider them a sort of friend. Death was never hidden from me my whole life. My parents brought me to funerals as a child. I lost all my grandparents before turning ten. As a middle schooler, I altar served funerals nearly every other week for our local church. So in a way, I was familiar with Death and its ways. My inner child would tell you that this was not a traumatizing experience during my childhood, rather, it made me realize the natural course of life. I understood why some people were present and some weren't.

I think Death is someone we <u>all</u> need to grow familiar with. Not in a way that makes us calloused to the pain of others or the senseless deaths we see on the news, but rather a familiarity that changes our outlook on life.

When you are familiar with Death and keep it in your awareness, when you think of it as walking beside Death each day, you will begin to notice a lot more about your life. Many of my favorite books have some of these underlying messages and tones, and I know my newfound opinion has shaped a lot of what I write.

For example, in *Fire* by Kristin Cashore she says, "If we knew a person was going to die, we'd hold harder to the memories." I think of that sometimes—the idea of not knowing. If I knew my birthday dinner the Sunday before my birthday was the last time I would hug my father good-bye, would I have reacted differently? Would I have cherished the moment more? I sure believe so now that I have time to reflect back.

In the *Crescent City* series by Sarah J. Maas, Bryce notices the message about Memento Mori, "Remember that you will die, and enjoy each pleasure the world has to offer." If we know that Death is close, how much more will we enjoy the smallest parts of our human lives?

In some ways, people might say thinking this way is morbid. I have gotten a lot of concerned looks with my somewhat casual acceptance of Death at this "still young" point in my life.

In my eyes, though, this way of thinking cannot be more freeing. It's not morbid, it's a comfort of living my life but knowing every moment could be my last. When you have an awareness of Death, especially your own, the clock feels on. I'm not afraid to go after my biggest dreams, and I won't give in to anxiety for long, because I know

I want to see this dream through before my time is gone. I don't take a single day for granted because I know tomorrow is not guaranteed. Can I tell you how amazing it feels not to be held back by things other people would find to be the chain that drags them down to the bottom of the ocean floor?

What if you could turn the weights of your life into life vests?

Cancer was my knock in the head—the thing that pushed this home through my thick skull. Because in those months I was scared. I was afraid this time would end without having truly lived it. So I fought, and I came back bigger, better, and stronger than before. In my own time, I stepped into my own. I have settled this in a healthy way.

I want to live a long and full life. I want to grow and build something wonderful. I want to publish entire series of books. I want to have a family and be able to set them up for success in their own lives.

I am going to fight for this every day with Death by my side—a companion that I can say "not today" to as they smile and let me keep living. When it's finally my time, I hope it's like an embrace and a "welcome home" as they guide me on to a place beyond this one.

Let Death be your Life's Greatest Teacher.

Death is not your enemy. Death is a guide, a mentor, a friend. Most importantly, Death is a reminder to look at your life with warmer eyes.

You don't have to always be happy. You don't need to love your suffering. If suffering becomes too much, you need to turn to your party members and let them help you see the path through the dark forest.

In those horrible two years, I sometimes felt it all was too much to handle. I don't care how positive my outlook is. There were moments where I thought I was going to unravel. It's in those moments that you hand your suffering to someone else to help you carry it. For me, that was Leona. She is both a vampire hunter and healer, which is a lot of responsibility. It is probably very taxing both mentally and physically to be around pain and death so much, day after day. However, it made her the perfect person to lift me up when I was suffering.

Welcome Death as your friend. Look on the small moments with gratitude. See the silver lining. Believe that the sun will come out tomorrow. Hope for a better, kinder world. Be the light in the darkness. Shed positivity wherever you go, however you can, even when it's hard. Ultimately, take action because the fairytale you seek to build deserves it.

In our progress here, let's also make Death a little less literal. What happens when the unexpected happens? Which it will. It has happened in the past and it will happen again in the future. If you run into a setback in the pursuit of the everyday fairytale you have set in Chapter 11, what are you going to do? What if this Death is really just a failure? Are you going to throw in the towel? Or are you going to take a deep breath and then step forward for another opportunity to grow even stronger?

Unlike your character in this story or in a video game, we don't get a second chance at life. Death is far more permanent. The funny thing is that the fear you probably live with instead is a lot less permanent. You can choose to say, "I'm not afraid of Death because I'm living my life to the fullest I am capable of at the moment."

So, the choice is entirely up to you.

Even if you fail a few times along the road, don't let your fairytale die. Not while you still can draw the breath to fight for it.

SESSION RECAP:

It's time for a little Memento Mori of our own. This session recap can be intense, especially if you've never paused to think about Death too much. Give yourself the space to fear, to grieve, to cry. I promise Death is a friend and looks on you only with kindness. So, pull out your journal and consider these next questions.

1. What would you be upset you did not achieve or get to do if you left this world next week?
2. Is there any person that comes to mind that you would have wished you spoke to one last time?
3. What would you do with your final days? Gatherings with friends? A walk on the beach? A crazy trip of a lifetime? Just cuddle your dog?

SIDE QUEST:

Reflect a little bit more on your answers to question three. If that's what you would do in your final days, why aren't you doing more of that now?

How can you begin to LIVE MORE every day? Without giving in to the "go crazy and quit your job" way, of course. What's something simple you could begin to do to live your life to the fullest?

Did something specific come to mind?

If so, GO DO IT.

Make those plans with friends, run to the other room and squeeze your pet, head out for a walk with your partner, call your mom, the list is endless.

Life is good and all around you, so go take advantage. Don't forget to appreciate the moment just a little bit more. Hug a little longer. Dig a little deeper. Because these are the moments that matter.

Noise and sensation come back to you slowly like you are approaching from down a long, dark tunnel. You shed the warm cloak that you had drawn around your body. You turn your eyes back to the sun. You feel yourself running, but it's all in your head.

Your eyes blink open as you sit up, and at first the world all around is blurry.

"Bless the gods," you hear Orik mumble.

Then they all come into focus. Your traveling crew. Your friends. The vampire hunter, Leona, and her companion, Rao. There are tears in all their eyes.

You cough as Leona and Rao's hands leave your body. The light of the spells they were dumping into you fades. They both sag back, looking sweaty, gaunt, and exhausted, but there is relief and satisfaction in their eyes.

"You...died..." Nemirah chokes out.

"Think you're getting rid of me that easily?" you garble out through a parched throat and dry mouth.

Orik pushes a canteen of water to your lips. "Hush!"

Priorities Change,
Time to Readjust

"But I will not run. I wouldn't be standing
here if I'd quit every time something seemed
impossible to overcome. I will not die today…"

FROM VIOLET SORRENGAIL IN
REBECCA YARROS' FOURTH WING

Throughout the rest of the night you cross in and out of consciousness. Your sleep is surprisingly deep and undisturbed. You had expected that pain might have kept you awake since the vampire had tried its best to rip out both the organs along your stomach and your very throat.

However, with the careful, thorough tending from not only your crew, but also Leona and Rao, you find that no one lets you go without a healing spell or potion long enough to start feeling it.

Leona and Rao have assessed your entire body for bites and have assured you and the others that the wounded creature had never used its teeth.

As you sleep, there isn't even fear to awaken you as if from a nightmare.

You know you are safe, surrounded by companions as well as a bright fire. Even thinking back to that moment when you lost your life, you don't feel a searing panic. It happened too fast for that. It was pain; then it was the light and the movement toward the beyond.

When you wake, it's morning. Leona is gone, but Rao still sits with Nemirah near the fire, finishing stirring a pot with a fragrant, herbal liquid.

"Ah, easy," he says to you as he sees you stir. "You may not feel it, but your body is still beat up."

Jonathan tucks his hands under your armpits to help you sit upright.

Rao pours some of the hot liquid into a cup, and then crosses over to you. He waves his hand over the steam to cool it before he hands it to you. "Drink this. It will help." You make an anxious face so Rao gestures for you not to worry. "It's just tea. I will put the rest in a canteen once it has cooled so you can take it with you. Drink a sip every few hours."

"Should I be nervous?" you ask as you sip the liquid. You wouldn't call the taste unpleasant, but it is certainly like sipping on grass.

"Vampire claws aren't an issue like the venom in their fangs is, but for a lot of people the wounds can still have additional…side effects. This should help you avoid that."

"So no turning into a vampire?"

"Nah, you're good." The smile that touches Rao's mouth is sweet, but a little sad.

You hear the jingle of a bell from a distance, and a few moments later Leona returns to the clearing, leading the cow. "There better be a good reason you ran sprinting after this heifer. Literally ran into a thicket just to avoid me."

"Worth ten silver?" Orik smirks at you.

Leona's jaw drops. "Ten silver? A bloody bounty for a cow?"

"A pregnant cow," you argue. "The farmer needs her back."

Leona laughs but shakes her head as she ties the cow to the back of the cart. "I could have bought you a cow for that much. Hell, you could have even convinced me to donate to the cause."

"Who knows?" you quip. "This one could be magical."

Leona literally leans on the cow's hindquarters. "I sure hope so."

"Give it up, Leona." Rao waves a hand at her. "Not everyone's—"

"No," you answer. Your eyes meet Leona's seriously before you continue. "You're right. It was foolish of me to run off like that. You all expended a lot of magic on my behalf. If you hadn't been here, nothing could have been done. I would have died for ten silver."

Leona crosses the cleared space and kneels before you. Her hand captures your own. "There are a lot of worse reasons to put yourself in harm's way. That farmer is going to be happy to have his cow, his livelihood back." She drops an extra ten silver into your hand.

"I can't take your money." You look up at her with surprise, but she waves you off.

"Take it. It will be put to better use than what I've been doing with it the past few years." Leona stands up and straightens, assessing the crew. "Don't let a poor farmer with probably a single cow struggle to pay you."

The beautiful thing about a "death" in a video game or an RPG campaign, is the ability to respawn, which we will be exploring more in the next chapter. Not only does it give you another chance to tackle the problem or the quest, but it also gives you a moment to rethink the method with which you were pursuing your goals (or maybe even the goal itself).

In real life, we of course are going to tell that big, final meeting with Death to shove off and happen at a much later date.

However, the way I want you to think about Death in the capacity of this book, is more like a failure. En route to our goals and our biggest dreams, we are going to experience failures all along the way. The good news is we always have a choice. We can accept failure and let it knock us down or eliminate us from the fight. Or, we can accept failure as a place to re-evaluate and move forward.

By treating our failures as little roadmap moments, we provide for ourselves built-in opportunities to realign with ourselves and with our goals. We get to decide if we want to try again, try something different, or change course. That is the beautiful thing about our journeys! There are always opportunities to adapt.

Trying to think positively during a moment of failure is really hard, near impossible. For example, there is a large percentage of aspiring realtors who fail the test on the first try when attempting to get their license. Seeing that score that doesn't make the journey move forward is incredibly saddening. One might think that they failed at studying, or that they are not smart enough to pass. In the end, we know that this sort of limiting thinking isn't going to help them move toward what they really want—which is likely starting their own business and becoming a real estate entrepreneur.

So, you need to put in the work now to be aware of those failures before they arrive. You need to develop a strategy for coping with the failure, as well as methods to reset if and when they happen.

With my realtor example above, this may be planning a really nice meal out whether or not you receive the result on the test that you want. You plan then, after enjoying the delicious food, to go online and schedule your next attempt at the test for one month later. This immediate deadline won't let you languish in disappointment for too long, because there is hope in the next chance. Then, you will strategize on how to not receive that result again. Did you study enough? Be honest with yourself. Do you need to learn in a different way? Would a group class or study session help? Would videos or flashcards show it to you in a new way?

This is how we have to start to think about our failures.

They are not going to hold us down, hold us back, or make us give up. They are platforms that are going to propel us forward in the future.

Having a plan to think this way ahead of time can help you make incredible strides toward your goals, because very little will take you by surprise.

Even when the surprising happens, you won't be asking yourself 'what now?'

Instead, you will look at a sheet of paper and say—this is what I do when the roadblock happens. How empowering!

The truth is, sometimes we need fantasy to survive reality. If we think back to our favorite characters, especially the one that you chose to walk along with you on this journey, you know that even when they experienced a setback, it didn't set them back for long.

SESSION RECAP:

Turn to your trusty companion guide or to your journal, because it's time to brainstorm. I think you are ready for this one because you have been doing the hard work already on this journey.

At your current trajectory toward your everyday fairytale, what is going to stand in your way? What are the roadblocks? What are your personal hang-ups?

Dig deep and think about this seriously.

Is there a week coming up where you know you are going to be crazy busy and your progress toward your goal is going to be put on pause?

What is your plan for adapting during that week? Are you going to logically plan ahead that you are going to do NOTHING toward your goal in that week? If yes, will you give yourself 100% guilt-free peace to do that? Are you going to lessen the to-do list toward the goal during that week instead? For example, if you committed to exercise three times a week, would two or one suffice?

Plan ahead. You will be surprised how roadblocks and failures become blips on a much larger map of success.

SIDE QUEST:

Colleen, how can you be so damn positive all the time? How can you look at failures with such openness? How do you not let it drag you down?

Honest answer: I'm not always perfect. I get down, sad, upset, depressed, jealous, and angry. On bad days, I consider throwing in the towel.

However, I have started to develop awareness. I recognize when I am experiencing those emotions, and I openly name them just like my vampires. Ah yes, I am feeling jealous of a fellow screenwriter who got an opportunity I was passed over for. Oh, feeling super sad today for no reason but that I feel my big dream is unattainable. My partner will literally hear me say these words out loud to him.

By acknowledging what I am feeling, I let myself *truly* feel. I know exactly why I feel the way I do. Then, I am able to redirect my energy, or just give myself a pass and say it will be a better day tomorrow. Overall, I have always found that time heals most things.

There is, though, one surefire way to feel your life is worthwhile in the difficult moments, and that is to help someone else when you are feeling down. Just like Leona going off to find the cow even after probably a long night of tending your wounds, when I am helping others, I see myself as part of a wider picture. When fighting so hard for our own personal fairytale, it will become very important to remain aware of the other people in the world—and the fairytales that *they* fight for.

So, when you hit a roadblock, take a step away and try to help someone else. This can be as small as paying extra attention to your partner or doing a chore for them that they had planned on doing. This could be signing up to assist a local charity or participating in a fundraiser.

So you have two choices for side quests in this chapter.

1. Make yourself a note on whatever your tracking system is that says: "Roadblock Checkpoint: Help someone else!" This will remind you to take that action when the going gets tough.

2. If you are feeling up to it, do something for someone else right now. Pass on a bit of kindness and help in this dark world. Because we all deserve to be supported in our fight for the fairytale.

You blink up at Leona. "Thank you."

A beautiful smile gleams down at you, illuminating a face that likely would win hearts in every direction if it wasn't always scowling and hunting down vampires.

What Leona said rings in your head again. *There are a lot of worse reasons to put yourself in harm's way.* She is right, you realize.

You had set out to embark as if on a quest, searching for adventure, perhaps searching for fame and fortune. Heck, you had taken that bounty more for the money and to prove to your new friends that you weren't afraid to take one.

Now, as you sit, you realize the deeper meaning behind the bounty. You don't know, but that cow could be the farmer's entire livelihood. Ten silver could be everything to their name—willing to give you everything to return their animal.

It doesn't make you rethink what you are doing, but it does make you rethink <u>why</u> you are doing it.

You realize that it was the way that you pursued your goal that brought about your own demise. Because in the end, the goal was right. The method was just wrong. If you had collected the crew and gone off after the cow together, or even waited until morning and followed the trail as Leona likely did, you might have been successful, and not have paid a steeper price.

LEVEL EIGHTEEN - RESPAWN

A New Lease on Life

> *"Being weak is nothing to be*
> *ashamed of…staying weak is."*

FROM FUEGOLEON VERMILLION IN PIERROT'S
ANIMATED TV SERIES BLACK CLOVER

After you have all eaten breakfast and Leona and Rao said their second set of good-byes before disappearing into the forest, Jonathan and Nemirah work to ready the cart while Orik sits beside you.

"What do you think?" he asks you. "Do you want to head back? We can settle your bounty with the farmer, return the cow, and get you back home? Or you could go work with Lila? Knowing your skills as a healer, she would be more than happy to have you around the shop. Maybe she could turn it into a full blown apothecary."

For a moment, you sit in silence. You're not quite sure what you want to do, but there is a tingle in your chest that tells you both of the options that Orik just offered are not the right one.

There was a reason that sitting around waiting for an injured patient with Morgana wasn't the best fit for you. There is not a single bone in your body that wants to throw in the towel now that you have gotten a taste for adventure.

"No," you finally say. "Let's continue. There is so much of this world I haven't seen."

Orik smiles with understanding. "Got a taste for it now, have you? Danger?"

"Not danger," you admit. "I have no desire to face off again with Death any time soon. But, I gotta say, seeing that cow and knowing we are going to fix something that's wrong in the world, feels pretty right."

The dwarf before you chuckles. "You're going to turn our crew into a bunch of do-gooders, aren't you?"

"Ah, come on," you laugh. "We'll let Jonathan have his trysts and flings. We'll help you impress Lila time and again. Nemirah can do her assassin stuff."

The sound of booted feet pauses before you. You look up into Nemirah's eyes.

"How did you know that?" she asks.

For a moment, a stone drops into your stomach. You gulp down a heavy swallow. "With your knife skills and your secretiveness…it was a guess." Her head tilts, cocks at you, and you can tell she is accessing every line of your face for a lie. "Honest. I don't know anything."

She nods, seemingly satisfied.

You swat yourself internally, but you can't help the words that spring to your lips. "So, that's really what you do? Are they bounties? Or—"

For a moment, Nemirah's serious features make you pause. Then Orik stands and nudges her as if to say, "Tell 'em."

Nemirah sighs. "I'm part of a group of assassins based out of Kahln. It's a society that anyone can join, but most of us are press-ganged into participation because we hold a debt of some kind to one of the leaders."

"A debt?"

Nemirah nods. "I owe more gold than most of the bounties I could earn in a year. That's why Orik and Jonathan let me claim the biggest bounties we complete. It helps me chip away...at the debt."

"So we are going to Kahln..."

"To make a payment."

There is a fold to Nemirah's shoulders that makes your heart clench.

In my own personal life, I find a lot of motivation in reading fantasy books or watching TV shows or movies during the training sequences. Though this may be just a little stepping stone in the wider plot, I find myself thinking about these for weeks if not months after, every time that I step into the gym.

As a lover of heavy weightlifting, it normally makes me laugh, because the characters in these stories are always running. If you asked me to do that, I would be miserable and on the ground after a few miles. Like literally in *The Lord of the Rings: Two Towers*, Aragorn, Legolas, and Gimli feel like they are running for the first thirty minutes of the movie. I can't imagine what it must have been like for their actors (or perhaps stunt doubles) to run for that long over that terrain. But, it definitely is inspiring.

I felt the same way with Nesta's 10,000 stair goal and Violet's sparring and dragon riding. This was more than honing one's body. This was about honing one's mind. A lot of that reflects in what you are doing here in this book.

It is not just about the goal and the steps that you will take to get there, but rather it is about the mindset that you develop when trying to reach that goal. Because fighting for the fairytale never ends. In order to accept that, you need to have a mind that can bounce back from problems and push you ever toward the future.

Everything that we are working on here is teaching you not to be weak…but not necessarily in a physical sense (though your goal could absolutely be fitness related). It is about training our minds not to be so.

That is why leaning on our favorite characters is so important, because even though their lives are not perfect, just like ours, the characters in stories have planned character arcs. Thank you, writers! In the most satisfying stories, flawed characters learn their lessons and reap the rewards that follow from making better choices or being better people. That is why in the fight for your fairytale, you must consider your own character arc and make a strategy to plot it out.

Have you always considered yourself "a poor student," "unable to finish things," "lacking self control," or any other number of limiting descriptions? Have you ever wished to be the opposite? If that is the case, then you are starting to see a bigger, wider fairytale.

It is not just about achieving a goal, it is about changing who you see yourself as in the process. For example, in my own story, I always knew I was a talented writer. I knew I had the capability to write stories that people enjoyed. I knew I was a skilled communicator. However, when it came to my passion stories, I labeled myself as someone "unable to finish the story." For many years, it was utterly debilitating when it came to pursuing the fairytale. As you have heard before throughout this book, I actively got in my own way.

It took cancer and following this process of trusting Leona for me to begin to re-label myself. Yeah, I didn't finish stories in the past. Now, I am seeing things through to the end. I'm going to set deadlines. I'm going to get the support of others. And I am going to make things happen.

As I began this big adventure in my fairytale, I failed along the way. I missed self-imposed deadlines. I made up excuses. I found other things to do to fill my time, but I kept checking in. I kept turning to Leona. Eventually, my mindset about myself started to shift. I saw I was capable and I never turned back.

Now, I have confidently "finished" two screenplays in two years of graduate school that are ready for the industry. You are reading this, so that means I finally finished a book.

I can tell you, that means there is more to come, because now the floodgates are opening. By breaking down my dream into smaller goals that I have not only achieved but rewarded myself for, I know I can do it again, and again. You know how someone becomes a full-time writer? They write stories and finish them, again and again. One story at a time.

As you complete your everyday fairytale and move on to a bigger adventure of your own, so, too, will you be proving to yourself that you can do something hard. It is going to make every step of the journey moving forward an easier one.

SESSION RECAP:

The next chapter is going to be all about expanding your fairytale, but I want you to be fully ready for the step when it comes. So this session recap is going to be key. You may want to look back at some of your early personal character work in Part One. You may want to think about how your everyday fairytale fits into a larger picture.

Consider these questions and reflect on them in your companion guide or journal.

1. Who do you say that you are? Is there dissonance between that person and who you want to be?
2. What stands in your way of being that person?
3. Is your current everyday fairytale a stepping stone to a larger one that would transform who you are as a person? If not, what sort of goals would you need to pursue to become that person?

SIDE QUEST:

Since we are going to be moving forward taking A LOT of pointed action that may be daunting very soon, in this respawn point, I want you to go back through this book and re-do one of the activities from a previous chapter that you enjoyed.

To give you a quick reminder:

Level One - Take a walk in nature

Level Two - Clean one tiny mess

Level Three - Throw tennis balls or flick sticky notes

Level Four - Ask family & friends what they love about you

Level Five - Put away any shiny objects that have crept back into your space

Level Six - Collect and/or utilize a health potion

Level Seven - Put yourself in a new situation / Try something new

Level Eight - Tell others you are grateful for them and why

Level Nine - Watch a movie with a character you love

Level Ten - Find a cool photo of the comfort character walking alongside you

Level Eleven - Shoot me an email update

Level Twelve - Connect with someone in the Discord server

Level Thirteen - Refresh your tracking system (color code, expand, rewrite)

Level Fourteen - Add a few more rewards to your system

Level Fifteen - Axe another vampire if possible, if not, just name them

Level Sixteen - Do something you would do in your last week on earth

Level Seventeen - Help someone else

Take action in any of these ways in any capacity that suits your energy at the moment. This is meant to help you feel good, so don't put any pressure on yourself. Make it fun! Enjoy the moment!

You push to your feet and kick dirt over what's left of the fire pit. "Then, let's go."

"What?" Nemirah asks.

"Let's go make your payment, so we can get on the road again. We can pick up more bounties. Heck, I'll let you take 75% of whatever I make if it will reduce your debt faster."

Orik trips over his pack as he starts to lift it. Jonathan turns back from the cart.

Nemirah stares.

They are all shocked. You can see it written on their faces.

Nemirah's face is downturned and cast in shadows. "You would do that…for me?"

You find your fists clenching. "Yeah, no one deserves to be forced to kill to pay back a debt."

"You don't even know why or how I got it."

"I don't need to know if you don't want to tell me."

You take a deep breath as you realize you mean it. Nemirah has become your best friend among the crew. She's smart, quippy, kind, and reliable. She's an amazing teacher. Without knowing a single thing, you know you would help her in any situation.

You step toward her and open your arms. An invitation for a hug, only if she wants one.

There is an awkward moment of silence. You start to rest your hands down.

Then, Nemirah crashes into you, clutching you close in a big, desperate hug that you suddenly realize you both needed.

Meeting Your Big (Brillant) (Expanding) (Goal)

> *"When people say impossible, they
> usually mean improbable."*

FROM NIKOLAI LANTSOV IN LEIGH
BARDUGO'S TV SERIES SHADOW AND BONE

You and Nemirah sit up front in the cart and guide the horse together down the other side of the mountain. Though you have wrapped your injuries up tight and have drunk your fill of healing potions, the jolts and bumps in the path sometimes make you wince as the cart rolls back and forth down the switchback trail lined on either side by pine trees.

Every so often, you catch Nemirah glancing at you sympathetically. "I'll be fine," you encourage her. "It already feels loads better."

"You're going to have some brutal scars," she says. She gestures to her own neck. You can't help but touch the rough bandage that currently circles your neck where Leona stitched and healed the pieces back together.

You shrug because as you think about it, you don't really mind.

"Scars are stories," Orik shares from the back where he fiddles with a pipe. "Best kind too."

"Only because you have loads of 'em," Jonathan includes. "Hey, maybe in town we could get you a tattoo to cover it up! In my opinion, *tattoos* tell the best stories. They are chosen artwork."

"If they mean anything at all," Nemirah laughs. "I think there's one on your back that you don't even remember getting one drunken night."

"I don't know," you say as you shift in your seat. "I'll have to see how they turn out. If they're cool, I'll keep them. If not, we'll cover them."

Jonathan nods. "Sounds like a plan to me!"

The entire cart falls silent again as the city of Kahln comes into view along the mountain range farther to the north. It's a ringed city built right into the side of the mountain. The lower reaches where the merchants and traders go to peddle their wares. The middle reaches where the colleges and guilds train the experts and skilled crafters of tomorrow. Then, the highest reaches where the leaders of the city gather and the temples to the gods line either side of the road.

From what Nemirah has shared, the assassin's guild sits in that second tier of the city. On the outside, it's a simple tavern, but through a few rooms and down a couple of passageways, one enters the bowels of the city. Among the sewer systems, the guild has carved out an entire city within the heart of the mountain. It sounds incredible and also absolutely terrifying. You're not sure if you want to see it or run far, far away.

To begin this chapter, I want to reflect on a little conversation between Frodo and Gandalf in J.R.R. Tolkien's *The Fellowship of the Ring*.

"I wish it need not have happened in my time," said Frodo.

"So do I," said Gandalf. "And so do all who live to see such times. But that is not for them to decide. All we have to decide is what to do with the time that is given us."

The time that is given us. That time is now.

In role-playing games, BBEG means Big Bad Evil Guy. It's the boss fight. It's the biggest challenge. It's likely what the player characters have been garnering experience to face off against this entire time.

In the Fight for Your Fairytale universe, BBEG means Big Beautiful Expanding Goal. It's our boss fight. Our biggest challenge. It's our biggest adventure. It's likely what you will be working and training for the rest of your life. It's the fairytale, and it will always be expanding.

The more that you work toward crafting a beautiful life, a fairytale of your own making, the more you will want to be a part of it. You are going to entrench yourself. Your work will be found in every small piece and tiny crevice. You will be the fairytale and it will be you. It's going to be hard to differentiate one from the other.

As we make our way toward that beautiful scenario, know that it's going to take trial and error to find what feels right. It is going to take adapting. What you think might be your fairytale today might become totally different tomorrow, and that's awesome!

However, for now, we are going to set aside the side quests to home in on our current big adventure. Perhaps if you like the tiny bites of the side quests, you will plan a few side quests that together will bring you closer to the goal of your big adventure. I love breaking goals up in this way! Make a bounty board and complete all the bounties for an amazingly big, connected success!

The big adventure should be 1000% daunting. It should scare you a little. You shouldn't know all the steps it will take to get there. Most importantly, though, it should excite your heart in a way nothing else does. If you're anxious about this new BBEG yet also can't stop thinking about it, then you are on the right course.

There are so many ways to build a fairytale that there is no way I can give examples for everything. To give you a sense of scope, I am going to mention a sample BBEG based off of where I currently am in life.

As a young couple about to embark on the adventure of marriage, my partner and I are excited by the prospect of buying our own house. It doesn't have to be big. It doesn't have to be fancy. It just has to be our own. We are excited for the chance to paint the walls and dig around in the backyard, all things we cannot currently do as renters—that's not allowed in the lease!

If buying a home is our current BBEG, then we have to break down the steps to get there, because that's not something we can do overnight!

Here are a few sample side quests and habits we are going to have to implement to get there:

- Talk to a mortgage lender about how much we can afford

  ▷ Discuss first-time homebuyer programs for deals or discounts

    ▷ Discuss down payment and how much we should collect beforehand

    ▷ Discuss budget ranges and get real about what that looks like in a house

- Save money for a down payment

    ▷ Set aside x% of our paychecks each month

    ▷ Research high interest savings accounts to place the money in

    ▷ Celebrate each time we contribute to the account

- Talk to a realtor about potential options in the cities we love

    ▷ Consider other areas or nearby cities, make a list

    ▷ Consider purchasing a new construction or a fixer upper, pros and cons

    ▷ Consider what it would look like to go small—a conversation between my partner and I about what's really a non-negotiable

As you can see in my example, if the BBEG is buying a house, the goal should be broken down into smaller and more manageable tasks. Then, these side quests should be given even smaller stepping stones, little actions that you can tangibly complete and also give yourself a reward for doing.

You have worked hard and built yourself up to this point, so don't be afraid. Dive in with an open heart. Let's explore what your BBEG could look like together.

SESSION RECAP:

Open your journal to a brand new fresh page. We are going to need something wide open. A clean slate, a fresh start.

Set a timer for ten minutes, and just like we did for the "Wouldn't it be cool if…" list, you are going to jot down any big goal that comes to mind. Don't limit yourself, because by seeing all the big goals, we are going to start to home in on the right one. It's okay to want a ton out of life, so if you can, fill the page. Even if you just end up with one or two, this exercise will be a success!

Put each goal in a little thought bubble. We're making a mind map—a visual organizational tool used for brainstorming, planning, and note-taking.

Once that timer goes off, sit back and look at your map. Do any of the words or phrases pop off the page to you? Are there any you feel drawn to? These emotions are key to home in on.

If you don't feel anything stands out, what would you enjoy trying first? Remember, this isn't the end-all-be-all for the rest of your life. It's just something you are working toward now. If you end up finding it's not right, we'll look back at this map, or craft a fresh one, repeat the process and go from there.

Okay, scary time, pick one.

Grab a highlighter and color over the BBEG you are going after first! Ah, there it is on the page, glaring at you now! Does it feel good? Does it feel a little nerve-wracking? Great!

Now, turn to the next clean page. In the center of this one, you are going to copy the word or phrase that you highlighted and put another thought bubble around it.

From what's in your head right now, what are some of the big side quests you would need to complete to reach this BBEG? You might even need to put topics to research to learn more! Put those words or phrases in a differently shaped bubble with lines connecting them to the BBEG.

Lastly, what are the little to-dos you have to accomplish within each of your side quests? Get small. Get nitty gritty. What S.M.A.R.T. activities will you be doing to receive a reward toward your side quest?

Give yourself as much time as you need to brainstorm this. Channel everything that you have learned about yourself and about this process in this book. Have fun with it! You are a mighty explorer, and your next adventure is going to be amazing.

SIDE QUEST:

Back in Level Thirteen, I mentioned there was a third option toward tracking your goals that you might be interested in and that might involve a spreadsheet. If this interests or excites you, let's explore it. If not, you can absolutely skip this side quest in favor of charting out your BBEG, side quests, and mini tasks using the methods we explored in Level Thirteen. Go with your gut and what feels best. You don't need to suddenly come to love spreadsheets if you hate them.

Option C: A really cool spreadsheet

What if you tracked your progress toward your personal goals, your BBEG, just like the XP (experience points) of an RPG campaign or video game? If you take the little tasks within your side quests and assign each a certain number of experience points, you will be able to "level up" as you complete them.

I like this idea because I like concrete tracking. I like planning ahead, and I like to see the meter fill up as I get closer and closer to the next level.

The spreadsheet is pretty simple. Just like in a video game, you need a certain number of experience points to reach the next level. So, for example, to get to Level Two, you will need to accumulate 300 XP. However, to get from Level Two to Level Three, you will need 900 XP. And so on.

You will find a downloadable template for this in Google sheets format on my website by going to colleenochab.com/fairytaleresources. It is already formatted with formulas and calculations, so all you need to do is fill as you complete your goals. There are other pages within the spreadsheet as well for you to break down rewards when you reach each new level or complete a certain task.

Check it out!

Staring down at Kahln, your heart still beating fast thinking about the assassin guild's underground city, you ask Nemirah a question without thinking twice.

"Once you pay off your debt, would you stay in the guild?"

Nemirah considers the question. "I don't know. It is a good way to make coin, but after everything, after how they played me when I was weak, I don't think I want to see them ever again."

You nod in agreement, but then find a different fear bubbling up inside your chest for your friend. "Will it come back to haunt you? Is there a penalty for leaving the guild?"

Nemirah shakes her head. "If I leave on good terms, they won't do anything. But I don't think you can ever actually *leave* the guild. You're just an inactive member."

"So they might reach out to you again? For another job?"

"Maybe." Nemirah grips the horse's reins a little tighter. "When that happens, though, it will be my decision to take it. Not theirs."

The pride and determination in Nemirah's eyes make that fire in your heart burn a little brighter, like it's stoking a flame.

What's Your Next Fairytale?

"I walk beside you because warriors walk together."

FROM COLLEEN OCHAB IN HER DEBUT BOOK
FIGHT FOR YOUR FAIRYTALE
(AND PROBABLY SOMEONE ELSE BEFORE ME...
BUT JUST LET ME CLAIM IT FOR THIS INSTANT)

Nemirah pulls the cart to a stop a few hours later in front of a simple homestead far on the outskirts of the city's farming lands. There is a wide yard bordered with a rickety fence that holds a wild, near overgrown garden. In the back, a small barn, probably more of a shed with an extended covering attached, leans haphazardly. A donkey brays from its shade, running to the fence blocking it from going farther.

"Quiet, Jennie!" a voice shouts from within the house. "What's got you all riled up?"

The farmer appears in a loose-fitting work shirt and gray trousers with patchwork repairs. A straw hat sits at an angle over the gray hair on his head. His skin is wrinkled with both age and sun. He walks with a minor limp.

You step down from the cart and move to the back, working to untie the cow.

"Margarette!" the farmer exclaims. He rushes out toward you, giddy as a school child on holiday. His limp is all but forgotten. "Oh, bless you! She spooked in a storm and ran off for the mountains. I haven't seen her for weeks!"

The farmer presses to Margarette's side and holds her mighty head in his arms. He ducks his forehead to hers, cooing like he's soothing a child. The cow closes its eyes and nuzzles into his touch.

"How's that babe of yours?" the farmer asks the cow. "Still growing strong?"

You watch the farmer lean his head down toward the cow's stomach and listen as his hands inspect carefully with a familiar, expert touch.

When he finally stands upright, he seems to remember you are standing there. "Thank you so much! I owe you ten silver. Let me go get it."

You shake your head and shove your hand in your pocket where it crushes the bounty you took from the tavern those few short days ago. "No, no, we found it on our way to Kahln. We're glad she's home with you."

Tears rise to the corners of the man's eyes. "Please, let me compensate you for your trouble."

A laugh echoes inside your head. If only the farmer knew the trouble you went through to get his cow, but he doesn't need to know that. "It was no trouble at all."

The farmer nods. "Jennie was missing her something terrible." When you blink at him, the farmer gestures to the donkey. "They're best friends. Have been their whole life. My wife bought them both at an auction maybe five years ago. They haven't been separated since."

You smile at the farmer as he leads Margarette toward the barn. Jennie, the donkey, brays and trots back and forth along the fence until she can nuzzle the cow herself. The trio settles into happy silence and you separate yourself and head back to the cart.

I'm super excited that you have a new BBEG, a new big adventure, to pursue. Remember, building your fairytale and achieving your dreams can be both inside and outside of work. Happiness does not need to be found in your job, but rather, the life you build around it, the life your job makes possible. Check in and reflect often. If you chose to pursue a goal related to work this time, maybe next time you can pursue a goal that's entirely personal or important to your family.

Where you originally wanted to go may not be the ultimate destination, but luckily all the side quests along the way will help you realize, return to your compass, and hopefully have some fun along the way!

SESSION RECAP:

I know that to build your fairytale you are going to be doing a lot of fighting, so no side quest for you in this chapter, but I do want to do some reflecting together.

Have you noticed a deeper, underlying theme to the goals that you have been pursuing over the course of this book? Is there a deeper purpose behind your BBEG?

I am hoping the answer is yes, because in the end, our fairytale needs to have deep meaning. It's like the foundation that holds up a mighty castle.

If your goal is work related, maybe you want to create a steady financial footing for your family or prove your expertise in a community that might not yet welcome you fully.

If your goal is health related, maybe Death has whispered in your ear that you need to say "Not today" more loudly and with more confidence behind the words.

If your goal revolves around your mind or mindset, you've likely discovered that the voice inside your head is your only constant companion, and you want to be the one in charge.

If your goal revolves around your community, maybe you have realized that by serving others, you fill a hole in yourself.

For me, sharing a little bit of my cancer journey is the surface level goal of this book. It has been cathartic to describe in words some of the most challenging moments of my darkest forests. However, on a deeper level, I want everyone to know they are not alone. I want everyone to see suffering doesn't happen in a vacuum. I want everyone to see that we are each warriors and we should be walking together. I want positivity and kindness to fill our heads and our world instead of negativity and hate.

I know life's not always perfect like that, but at least I can choose to walk beside you—because that's my fairytale.

I am so grateful for the time you spent with me on this journey. I am excited to see where it leads all of us. I am grateful for the trust and the deep work that you put into it. I am grateful you have been able to meet Leona because I feel a little spoiled having her all to myself. I am grateful for the people who shaped this book and the ones who will be shaped by it. I hope it was fun. I hope it felt like an adventure. And ultimately, I hope it was a good story.

Thank you for fighting for your fairytale. Never stop.

You step back into the cart up front with Nemirah and fish out the silver that Leona gave you, passing her eight of the ten coins. "I promised you 75%, but take 80% since I had bounty beginner's luck."

Orik's and Jonathan's grins grow wide in the back of the cart.

"You really don't have to do this," Nemirah says as her fingers close around the coins.

"When I set out on my adventure, when I left home," you explain, "I didn't know where I was going or why. I just knew I wasn't where I was supposed to be and had an itch to get out. Now, no matter where the journey may lead or where the road may take me, I trust myself that I will make a good choice. And, I will be right alongside all of you."

Jonathan and Orik throw their arms around you both and pull you into the deepest of bear hugs. You clutch their arms and hug them back, pulling Nemirah close. Yes, this is right where you need to be.

THE ADVENTURE RECAP

Thanks for being part of my fairytale!

Extended Reading & Listening List

If you have grown interested in any of the properties that were mentioned in this book, please refer to this list broken down between non-fiction, fiction, and non-literary titles included.

Non-fiction books mentioned in this book:

Reflections on the Art of Living by Joseph Campbell

Rest Is Resistance: A Manifesto by Tricia Hersey

The Life Changing Magic of Tidying Up by Marie Kondo

The Untethered Soul: The Journey Beyond Yourself by Michael Alan Singer

Fictions (books and movies/TV shows) mentioned in this book:

A Court of Thorns and Roses Series by Sarah J. Maas

A Song of Ice and Fire Series by George R. R. Martin

Beauty & The Beast movie

Black Clover TV series

Crescent City Series by Sarah J. Maas

Dungeons & Dragons 5e by Wizards of the Coast

Fire by Kristin Cashore

Fourth Wing by Rebecca Yarros

Good Will Hunting movie

Harry Potter and The Sorcerer's Stone by J.K. Rowling

House of Dragon TV series

Pirates of the Caribbean: The Curse of the Black Pearl movie

Ranger's Apprentice Series by John Flanagan

Shadow and Bone TV series

Something Wicked This Way Comes by Ray Bradbury

Star Wars: Episode II: Attack of the Clones movie

The Chronicles of Narnia Series by C. S. Lewis

The Hobbit by J. R. R. Tolkien

The Hunger Games by Suzanne Collins

The Karate Kid movie

The Legend of Vox Machina TV series

The Lion King movie

The Lord of the Rings Series by J. R. R. Tolkien

The Witcher TV series

The Wonderful Wizard of Oz by L. Frank Baum

Non-literary properties mentioned in this book:

Balder's Gate 3 video game

Critical Role Podcast

D&D Beyond gaming platform

Hamilton musical

Legend of Zelda: Twilight Princess video game

Skyrim video game

Warhammer Vermintide II video game

I have also included a short reading list of some of the most impactful books that I have read that have either inspired my imagination or have helped me develop new goals to pursue but did not make the cut into the main portion of this book, even though they probably could have. These books are divided into both fiction and non-fiction categories.

Book Recommendations for Future Inspiration / Fight for Your Fairytale Endeavors

Non-Fiction:

Meditations by Marcus Aurelius

The Mountain Is You by Brianna Wiest

The Defining Decade by Meg Jay

Grit by Angela Duckworth

The Obstacle Is The Way by Ryan Holiday

Financial Feminist by Tori Dunlap

I Will Teach You To Be Rich by Ramit Sethi

Money for Couples by Ramit Sethi

Fiction:

The Book Thief by Markus Zusak

Throne of Glass Series by Sarah J. Maas

Legends & Lattes by Travis Baldree

Stories of Your Life by Ted Chang

Writing & Screenwriting:

Published by Chandler Bolt

Safekeeping by Chelene Knight

The Protagonist's Journey by Scott Myers

The 12 Week Year for Writers by A. Trevor Thrall

Acknowledgments

To my faithful editor, Kayleigh at Enchanted Edits, your dedication to this story is utterly incredible. Speedy, efficient, yet catching all my errors with commas! Thanks for being this story's final polisher!

To my invaluable beta readers, Bethany, Emily E., Emily M., Liz, and Natalie, as well as Amy, the licensed therapist that I consulted to make this book ring true for a wide variety of readers, your insights helped perfect every little detail in this book. Thank you for giving of your time and for the outpouring of love.

To my coaches Allison, Brittany, and Kerk and the entire team at SelfPublishing.com. You set my feet on the path to this book, and I will be forever grateful.

To my launch team and ARC readers, especially Kat, thank you for being the voices that shouted about this story to the world. We all need more cheerleaders like you!

To my amazing partner, Justin, who doesn't realize just how much preparing dinner and giving me time in the evening to write makes my soul feel loved. Thank you for believing in me!

To my mother, Kathleen, who endlessly supports me. Thank you for helping me pursue my dreams and walking with me along the journey. Woman to woman, you will always be my role model.

To my best friends, Ethan, Liz, and Melanie, for being my personal party members. Thank you for introducing me to Dungeons & Dragons, listening to all of my crazy story ideas, cheering me on every step of the way, and being the truest, most dedicated friends one could ask for.

To the team at Alexian Brothers Hospital Cancer Institute and Northwest Oncology and Hematology, most especially all of my amazing nurses and technicians, Lucy, Dr. Kanter, Dr. Rajendran, Dr. Godellas, Dr. Kapadia, and everyone who supported me along my breast cancer journey. Your care and compassion made me feel secure and sheltered during the storm.

To breast cancer, no one likes you, but thank you for breaking apart my life, causing a crisis, and showing me that life is too short. It is because of you that I finally followed my daydreams and took pointed action to becoming a writer. It is because of you that I fight for the fairytale every day. But just saying, don't show your face around these parts ever again.

To Mereoleona Valerien, I know you came out of my own mind, but you have so much depth that I can't really imagine you are something I created. I know you were put into my life for a reason. I will never cease to be grateful for the fact that you walk beside little old me when you have such a vast and awesome life to live. Here's to Becoming Chaos!

Interested in More?

Leona's eager to adventure with you.

Wondering how Mereoleona Valerien, the elven
druid, became a gruff vampire hunter?
Questioning who that one-armed stranger was in Lila's shop?

Find out in *Becoming Chaos*, an epic medieval fantasy full of Chaos,
witty sibling banter, and messy love triangles! Coming soon!

Giving Back: A Personal Quest

"Even the smallest person can change the course of the future."
– J. R. R. Tolkien, The Lord of the Rings

Fight for Your Fairytale was born from battle—written in the quiet moments between appointments, scans, and treatments at Alexian Brothers Hospital Cancer Center. That's where I fought for my own fairytale, and it's where many warriors continue theirs today. In honor of that fight, 10% of all profits from this book will be donated to cancer research and to support patients at the Alexian Brothers Hospital Cancer Center in Illinois. Your purchase doesn't just fuel your story—it helps others keep writing theirs. Thank you!
Our fight continues until cancer is gone.

About the Author

Colleen H. Ochab is a Chicago-based writer, screenwriter, and founder of Fight For The Fairytale Editorial, a developmental editing company that empowers fantasy writers to craft cinematic novels and screenplays. She holds an MFA in Screenwriting from DePaul University and, as a breast cancer survivor, believes we should all live boldly and chase our fairytales with courage–just like our favorite heroes. When she is not crafting characters, plots, and new worlds, Colleen enjoys weightlifting, traveling the world, and spending time with her amazing partner, Justin, as well as their rescue dogs. Whether you're crafting worlds on the page or rewriting your own life's narrative, Colleen believes in the power of storytelling to transform.

Will yours be next?

Thank you for reading the first of many fantasy adventures written by @colleenochab

You can follow her creative journey online where she posts regularly about her writing and filmmaking endeavors, as well as offers developmental editing tips for fantasy writers seeking to make their stories cinema-ready!

Fight for the Fairytale; it does exist.

Thank You For Fighting For The Fairytale With Me!

Your support means more than I can ever say. Every message, every bit of feedback—it's like a torch guiding the way through the dark forest. I love hearing what resonated with you, what sparked something magical, and even where the path could be clearer.

Your insight helps me grow this book—and the ones still to come—into even greater allies on your journey.

If you have two minutes, I'd be honored if you'd leave a review on Amazon and share your thoughts: colleenochab.com/ffyf-review

Thank you for walking beside me.

Our fight continues,
– Colleen H. Ochab